THE MEWAR CONSPIRACY

An Epic Saga of How the Rajputs Defeated Aurangzeb

RRASHIMA SWAARUP VERMA

An imprint of
Srishti Publishers & Distributors

Srishti Publishers & Distributors
A unit of AJR Publishing LLP
212A, Peacock Lane
Shahpur Jat, New Delhi – 110 049

editorial@srishtipublishers.com

First published by Bold,
an imprint of Srishti Publishers & Distributors in 2022

10 9 8 7 6 5 4 3 2 1

This is a work of non-fiction, based on the author's thorough research of Indian history. Some events have been fictionalised for dramatic effect. While due care has been taken to verify all information at press time, any inadvertent miss brought to notice shall be updated in the subsequent editions.

Printed and bound in India.

To all my readers,
Thank you for your love.
I write because you read.

A NOTE FROM THE AUTHOR

To say that I have thoroughly enjoyed writing this book would most certainly be an understatement. Writing The Mewar Conspiracy has been a tremendously rewarding experience for me. To have been given the opportunity to delve deep into this period of India's rich history, to bring that incredible era, those monumental events, those fascinating characters to life again, well, I cannot think of a bigger privilege for an author. And the process! Gathering the information, validating and revalidating it through multiple sources, understanding the motivations of the characters, stepping into that time and place. It has been immensely enriching, enormously gratifying in so many ways.

There are several wonderful people who have guided and supported me through this process and made it possible for me to share this beautiful story with all of you.

First and foremost, I want to thank my brilliant literary agent, Suhail Mathur of The Book Bakers literary agency, for his constant guidance, support and wisdom. He has been an intrinsic part of the journey of this book, every step of the way. I'd also like to thank him for designing such an enthralling book cover. Truly the best literary agent, mentor and friend an author can wish for, Suhail is Agent

Extraordinaire. My deepest gratitude to him for everything that he does. This book happened thanks to him.

My heartfelt gratitude and appreciation to the outstanding team at Srishti Publishers and Distributors. I'd like to extend a huge thank you to my publishers Mr. J.K. Bose and Arup Bose for the support and warmth they have always extended to me, as also for the constant faith in my work. It is an honour to work with you and I am truly grateful to you for giving me an opportunity to present this wonderful story to the world.

A huge word of thanks to the editorial team at Srishti Publishers. It has been a great pleasure and privilege to work with Chief Editor Stuti Sharma Gupta and my Editor Alisha Verma Chopra. Their guidance and inputs have been invaluable, and I have really enjoyed working with such a diligent and committed team on this book.

Someone once said, "The world is full of kind, generous people." And it really is. I first realized this when I was writing The Royal Scandal. This realization was once again validated while writing The Mewar Conspiracy. There were so many wise and learned historians, experts and scholars who came forward and supported me with the intense research that I conducted for this book. I especially want to thank Dr. Shankar Kumar (Dept of History, Hindu College, Delhi University), Diwan Gautam Anand (Writer, Sufi Poet and Hotelier), Salma Yusuf Husain (Persian Scholar and Historian) and Mr. Rajendra Singh (Ministry of Tourism (Govt of India) and Archaeological Survey of India) for sharing their deep knowledge and insights with me.

I would also like to thank all the channel partners for their dedication and commitment. Their seamless organization and management have been instrumental in bringing this book to its readers.

An enormous thank you to my family. My parents Shirley and Swapn, I love you so much. Thank you for all the incredible stories. You instilled a love for books in me and your support is precious beyond measure. My husband Puneet. You are my rock, the one I always depend on. I love you very much. And my son Eshan. You are my inspiration, my sunshine. You make me proud every day, my darling.

And now, from the bottom of my heart, I want to thank you, my reader, for believing in me. I hope you enjoy reading The Mewar Conspiracy as much as I have enjoyed writing it. This powerful tale of love, war and intrigue is a piece of my heart, and writing it has been one of the biggest privileges of my life. Intense, methodical research has gone into writing this book and you will find a comprehensive list of sources for your reference at the end of the book. Persian words have been hyphenated throughout the narrative as a stylistic regulation.

Once again, my deep gratitude. Your love and faith mean the world to me. I write because you read.

Chapter 1

1660, Kishengarh, India

The sun had been strong an hour before but now the horizon was a marvellous patchwork of white clouds and blue sky. The sound of laughter, the marble fountain spouting a steady stream of silver water, birds chirping. It was turning out to be one of those perfect afternoons. Made perfect still by the promise of rain in the air. And Princess Charumati loved the rain. It was a common sight to see her rejoicing its arrival with her female companions. With her lithe figure, long dark hair and graceful movements, the Princess looked beautiful, regal, seductive. But the rain brought that out in her. She waited for it all summer; still, it astonished her with its splendour when it finally came. Now, the tinkling of her silver *payal* and the swish-swish-swish of her *lehenga* as she danced with abandon, echoed off the checked marble floor and pristine white pillars that adorned the courtyard of the *zenana* palace. The palace was a part of the fort complex that had been built by her father seven years back. The fort was enclosed by a deep moated wall to protect it from enemy invasion, and the waters of Lake Gundalao[1] that surrounded the structure, were a sanctuary for all kinds of exotic birds.

"Soon the peacocks will appear." Charumati's best friend, Nirmal, left the rest of the group and walked over to the Princess. "How magnificent they are with those iridescent plumes. No wonder it is believed that they are created from the feathers of Garuda, Lord Vishnu's mount himself." She sighed and looked up at the sky. "This time of the year always reminds me of that story."

"Which story?" Charumati looked at Nirmal quizzically.

"The one in which Surya, the daughter of the sun god, falls in love with a peacock."

"That is a sad story." Charumati shook her head. "I prefer love stories with happy endings."

"Well, if you like happy endings, then perhaps you should write to him as soon as possible. Before your brother starts thinking about marrying you off to someone else. After all, Mewar and Kishengarh have not been on the best of terms since last year."

This was true. Like many other states, Kishengarh, too, had once been under the dominion of Mewar. However, after the conflict between Mewar and Akbar, Kishengarh became independent of Mewari rule. Last year, things had become particularly tense between the two states.

"Not to mention that he is considerably older than you," concluded Nirmal. She did not need to specify the name of the man she was talking about. There was only one man who had captured Charumati's heart.

"It will take more than that to keep me from marrying the only man I have ever loved." Charumati adjusted the pleats of her lehenga. "I can never forget the day I saw him at his coronation with baba. Strong, brave, handsome! Like a true *Suryavanshi* Rajput!"

"Well, considering that women do not usually attend public ceremonies, I must say that *Tau sa* treated you more like a son than a daughter."

"I am glad that he did. How else would I have seen the Rana?" Charumati placed her hand on her heart and sighed. "He looked so regal in his *poshak,* complete with *pagadi* and *kamarbandh* and the sword in his right hand."

"Oh Charu! I cannot understand how you can be so helplessly besotted." Nirmal laughed.

"How can you understand? You are not the one in love."

"That I am certainly not," agreed Nirmal.

"As Mirabai said, 'I am mad with love. And no one understands my plight. Only the wounded understand the agonies of the wounded.' Words that undoubtedly ring true."

Nirmal smiled. She couldn't blame Charu for being so much in love. Rana Raj Singh was special. He was the oldest son of Maharana Jagat Singh 1 and Maharani Medtaniji, the Princess of Marwar. His great grandfather was Amar Singh, the son of the brave and valiant warrior Maharana Pratap. Rana Raj Singh's lineage, though, was not the only reason that he was hailed and admired by all. Raj Singh was himself a courageous warrior and skilful ruler. Thoroughly adept at military matters, he was also competent at administrative ones. Charumati had first seen him at his coronation when he had succeeded the throne after his father's death in 1652. She had fallen in love with him instantly, vowing to marry him one day.

Just then, a maid appeared in the courtyard. She bowed her head. "*Rajkumari sa,* an old woman is at the palace doors. She wishes to see you."

"Is she asking for alms?"

"No, she is selling paintings."

"Paintings!" Charumati clapped her hands happily. "Oh, I would love to have a new painting to hang in my bedroom. Show her in at once!"

Five minutes later, a woman so old that she was almost bent over double, was being led toward the central courtyard of the palace. Even as she made her way toward the marble fountain where the Princess and her companions were congregating, Charumati couldn't help noticing that the woman was surprisingly nimble for her age. She was dressed in a simple *shalwar-kameez* and had a shawl draped around her head. She was carrying a heavy stack of paintings under one arm.

After greeting the Princess and her friends, the woman settled down on the marble floor of the courtyard. "I have many beautiful paintings to show you, Rajkumari sa," she said with a smile, revealing a set of heavily stained teeth. She removed the stack of paintings from under her arm, pulling out several portraits of emperors and kings. Not surprisingly, there were almost none depicting women, but then that was a consequence of *purdah*, a practice that protected women from public visibility.[2]

Charumati leaned forward enthusiastically, but as the minutes passed and the woman showed her painting after painting, she lost interest and looked bored.

"I do not like any of them."

The woman looked surprised. "These are genuine works of talent, Rajkumari sa. Each painting has very distinct brush strokes. You see, Mughal imperial patrons are very particular about individual styles. So much so that the fourth emperor Jehangir had even remarked, 'If there be a picture containing many portraits and each face be the work of a different master, I can discover which face is the work of each of them!' Such is the kind of detailing that you will find in these works."[3]

"I am not interested in all that." Charumati dismissed the woman's proclamations with a wave of her delicate hand. "Do you not have any of our brave and gallant Rajput kings?" After all, paintings were not just works of art. They were a representation of a ruler's ambitions, his legacy.

"No, I do not think I have any of the Rajput kings."

"That is a real shame!" Charumati looked at the woman indignantly. "Look again! And again, until you find one."

And so, the woman looked and looked, until finally she managed to pull out a painting with a gilded frame from the stack. She wiped the dust off it with the end of her shawl and held it up for the Princess to see.

"Here you are Rajkumari sa! This one is of the Maharana of Mewar. Rana Raj Singh."

Charumati's face lit up like a thousand diyas. Rana Raj Singh! The man she loved! And how regal he looked, in the traditional *achkan*, *churidar* and *turban*. He was holding a gold sword in his right hand and a lotus flower in his left. Beaming, the young Princess held her arms out for the painting.

"I am glad to have made you happy." The old woman handed the painting over and then turned to the stack again. This time, she effortlessly pulled out a painting from the top of the stack and held it up. "I am sure you would also like to take this one. The great emperor, Alamgir!"

All the girls gathered around the old woman, whispering and pointing to the painting. It was a large-sized one with a sparkling golden frame. The frame was covered in a turquoise and orange flowered motif design and the painting of the emperor had been done in profile. It was a full-length portrait, and he was dressed in bejewelled robes with the traditional halo of 'divine lights' behind his head that was characteristic of the Mughal rule from the reign of his grandfather, Jehangir.

With a smile, Charumati held her hand out. "Yes, I will take this too."

Nirmal looked at her in astonishment. As Charumati's best friend, she was aware of how much the young Princess detested the emperor. After all, everyone knew that Charumati's father, Raja Roop Singh, had died in a bloody battle at the hands of Aurangzeb himself. A favourite of Shah Jahan, Roop Singh, had fought many battles alongside him and had even accompanied an expedition to Afghanistan for which he had been generously rewarded. The warrior king had emerged victorious in several of these battles, but his luck seemed to have run out in 1658 and he was killed by Shah Jahan's younger son Aurangzeb, in the last battle he would ever fight. Charumati had loved her father very much and had even been his closest confidante and advisor. Her loathing for the Mughal emperor was understandable. Even though her brother Man Singh had accepted defeat and surrendered in front of the emperor to save his own life, Charumati's heart had been brimming with hatred and rage. Why then was she accepting a painting of the emperor? Nirmal tried to catch Charumati's eye, but the old woman had already placed the painting in the waiting arms of the Princess.

"You were wise to have acquired this painting." The woman nodded approvingly at Charumati. "The emperor is undoubtedly the mightiest of them all. It is no wonder he is called 'Alamgir' or conqueror of the world. Furthermore...."

Crash!

One minute the magnificent painting was in Charumati's arms and the next, it was lying on the marble floor, smashed into a thousand tiny pieces. Then, before any of the open-mouthed spectators could react or even utter a word, Charumati lifted her right foot and brought it down on what remained of the painting. Even as her bejewelled *jooti* made contact with the already shattered glass, crushing the emperor's face into even more minuscule smithereens, there was a collective gasp from all the women. Instant beads of perspiration appeared on

Nirmal's forehead as the full realization of what Charumati had done hit her.

"Rajkumari sa!" Shocked disbelief was etched across the old woman's face, as she stared at the smashed painting and then lifted her eyes to meet the young princess's mocking gaze. "Why did you do that?"

"To tell you and everyone else here exactly what I think of your emperor, your 'Alamgir'. In fact, I wish and pray that the emperor also meets the same fate, that he also gets crushed, finished, exactly the way this painting has been destroyed under the sole of my foot!"

"Charu!" Nirmal ran to her friend and grabbed her hands. "Take that back! Think of the repercussions!"

But Charumati was far too proud a Princess to take back her words. In any case, she had meant every word of what she had said. She detested the emperor more than anyone, so why should she not be honest about how she felt? She shook her pretty head and laughed.

"Take back my words! When did you ever hear of a Rajput doing that? My ancestors would return to haunt me. As it is, it is not my fault. It is hers. Why did she show me a painting of a man I so detest?" She pointed to the old crone. "What do I owe you for the two paintings? Name your price! Take twice the amount. The pleasure I got from crushing that painting under the sole of my foot is worth every penny spent!"

She turned to Nirmal. "Give her the money and send her on her way."

Then, she calmly adjusted the drape of her pink *odhni*, carefully picked up the painting of Raj Singh and walked away into the palace.

Bowing her head, the old woman picked up the stack of paintings and started shuffling out of the courtyard. But before she could walk even a few steps, Nirmal rushed to stop her.

"Wait! Let me pay you for the paintings."

She handed her a bag full of gold coins. The woman was surprised at the weight of the bag, but Nirmal pressed it into her wrinkled hands. Then, taking her by the arm, the young girl gently led the woman towards the shadier part of the courtyard. "It is a hot day and you look tired. Let me offer you a glass of *gulab sarbat*. Or would you prefer *chaas?* Come, let us sit under the shade of that *jamun* tree."

Five minutes later, a maid brought two silver tumblers filled to the brim with ice-cold chaas, garnished with mint leaves. Nirmal handed one of the tumblers to the old woman, who accepted it gratefully.

"*Meherbani,* sa." She gulped down the first glass quickly and then Nirmal handed her the second one. Her thirst partially quenched, this one she sipped more slowly, taking her time to savour the creaminess of the curd and the coolness of the mint. It was only once the empty tumblers had been taken away by the maid that Nirmal turned to her, with an anxious look in her eyes. Carefree by nature, Nirmal wasn't usually one to bother about trivial things, but even she understood that what had just happened wasn't in any manner trivial. She was actually amazed that Charumati did not understand or realize that. Even as she considered the best way to broach the subject, she couldn't help but notice that the shattered painting still lay on the marble floor, a sore sight that was plainly impossible to ignore. Nirmal cleared her throat.

"The Princess is young, far too young. And you would agree, would you not that nothing can be more hasty, more unthinkingly impulsive than youth?"

"Yes, that is true." The woman nodded her agreement.

"Sometimes we do things that we do not intend to. I am sure the Princess did not mean..."

She suddenly saw the woman staring admiringly at the necklace around her neck. This was nothing new. Most people stared at this particular piece of jewellery. It was difficult not to. The stunning peacock, elephant and floral motifs carved in gold and encrusted with pearls, rubies and *polki* rosettes unfailingly caught everyone's eye.

"That is a spectacular piece of jewellery," remarked the woman then. "A family heirloom, perhaps?"

In fact, the necklace *was* a family heirloom, dating back to the fifteenth century. It had been in Nirmal's family for several generations and had been given to her mother by her great *Dadi sa* before being passed on to Nirmal for her thirteenth birthday. She would pass it on to her daughter in turn and... Nirmal hesitated for just an instant before her hands went around her neck. She unclasped the necklace and, before she could change her mind, held it out to the old woman with a smile.

"It is yours."

The old woman looked shocked. Eyes widening, she frantically started shaking her head. "No, no! That is not what I meant."

Trying to smile, Nirmal placed the necklace into the woman's lap. "Accept it as a gift from me. Please, I will not take no for an answer."

The old woman lowered her eyes. "How can I accept this? You have already been so kind to me."

"You are our guest. And to us, a guest is like God." Nirmal leaned forward in her wooden chair. It was an outdoor *dhola maru* set, one of many that was used when someone wanted to sit out in one of the courtyards. Clearing her throat, she continued. "The Princess is also kind-hearted and generous. Like I told you, she must not have been thinking at that time. I would be grateful if you could disregard it as her childishness."

"Of course!" The woman patted Nirmal's hand. "The magnanimity and compassion you have shown toward a poor old woman like me has won my heart. Do not worry. Be assured that what happened today will most certainly stay between us. Not a word will be uttered outside the confines of this courtyard, I promise you."

She pressed Nirmal's hand one last time, as though re-iterating her commitment. Then she rose from her chair, laboriously picked up her stack of paintings and slowly shuffled toward the end of the courtyard. Nirmal's precious necklace was now tightly wrapped in the end of her thick shawl. Even as Nirmal watched her go, a sudden sense of urgency took over her senses, almost as though she could see something disastrous unfolding in front of her eyes, but didn't have the power to stop it. The other girls had all left by then and save for a pair of white pigeons who were pecking at the ground, looking for seeds and other food, Nirmal was alone. And then, just as the old woman exited the courtyard and finally disappeared from sight, a deafening clap thundered down from the open skies, announcing the arrival of the first rain. Nirmal looked up as huge, heavy drops of water pelted down on her. The rain they had all been eagerly waiting for had finally arrived. But this time, there was something different about the downpour. The sky had darkened considerably, the mellow blues and whites having given way to an ominous grey. It was almost as though the rain, too, was trying to deliver a message, attempting to tell them something.

"Do not overthink!" Nirmal chided herself. "Did she not promise that she would never utter a word to anyone? There is nothing to worry about, nothing at all."

Willing herself to believe it, Nirmal turned and walked back toward the palace door. As she passed by the marble fountain, a maid appeared with a broom in her hand. Even as she bent down to sweep away the pile of shattered glass that still lay there, Nirmal deliberately turned away, trying her best not to look at the remains of the painting that had been mercilessly smashed under the sole of Charumati's bejewelled jooti.

Chapter 2

Its strategic location had ensured that the city of Delhi had historically been the political centre of the Indian subcontinent for many a mighty empire. Of course, that also meant that Delhi was a city that had been destroyed and ruined several times, although only to be rebuilt over and over again. The Kuru, Mauryan, Kushan, Gupta, Vardhana, Gurjara-Pratihara, were the first empires to rule from Delhi, followed by the medieval Tomara and Chauhan dynasties which reigned from 736 to 1193. Then came about the formation of the Delhi Sultanate. The Mamluks, the Khaljis, the Tughlaqs, the Sayyids and the Lodis, in that order, were the five Islamic dynasties that ruled the subcontinent from Delhi. Finally, the Sultanate came to an end when the Mughal emperor Babur, defeated Ibrahim Lodi at the Battle of Panipat and firmly established the Mughal empire. Since the older Mughal rulers preferred to rule from Akbarabad, the city of Delhi subsequently went through a period of decline. Akbarabad, on the other hand, witnessed rapid development and building activity through the reigns and went on to become a thriving centre of art, architecture and religion, while Delhi was solely remembered for the former glory it had once possessed. Then the fifth Mughal emperor Shah Jahan, built the walled city of Shahjahanabad in Delhi in the year 1638.[4] Agra had developed a serious water problem[5], and the Mughal capital was shifted back to Delhi. Subsequently, when Shah Jahan fell ill with strangury in 1657, his son Aurangzeb captured and imprisoned him in Agra fort and was crowned the 'Emperor of Delhi'. While each of the Mughal emperors left his distinct mark, both from the unique policies he adopted as also from the success he enjoyed in expanding his rule around the region, if there was anyone who aspired to consolidate the Indian subcontinent under a single rule for the first time in history, it was the sixth Mughal ruler, Aurangzeb.

Born Muhi al-Din Muhammad in Dahod in the year 1618, Aurangzeb was the third son of Shah Jahan and his favourite begum Mumtaz Mahal. While Shah Jahan was a descendant of Emir Timur of the Timurid empire, Mumtaz Mahal was the daughter of a Persian nobleman. Aurangzeb was born during the reign of his grandfather Jehangir and received a noble education befitting a Mughal prince. Combat, military studies, Islamic studies, administration, literature, the young man had an astute understanding of all the subjects that a Mughal prince should have been proficient in. His primary aptitude, however, was for military roles and he proved his worth as a military commander early in his life, holding several strategic military posts during his father's reign.[6] His older brother Dara on the other hand, had a keen interest in fine arts, was a poet and was much more inclined toward a liberal and unorthodox bent of mind. The differences between the two brothers were palpable from the beginning,[7] and it was clear to anyone who saw them that they were the polar opposites of each other in every way. So much so that it sometimes seemed to their father that there was absolutely nothing that Dara and Aurangzeb would ever agree on.

The animosity between the two brewed for years, eventually turning into a bitter rivalry for the one thing, the one goal, that both had set their sights on. A goal that was as coveted as it was revered. The Jewelled Throne, also known as the *Takht-Murassa*. This supremely opulent throne had been built by Shah Jahan and had taken seven years to complete. Known to be modelled after King Solomon's *Takht-e-Sulaiman*, and covered with gold and precious stones from Shah Jahan's personal collection, the bejewelled seat of power was a masterpiece of Mughal workmanship, and it was believed that the ruler who occupied it was destined to be closer to heaven than earth.

Ya takht ya tubut.

Either the throne or the grave.

That was the order of the day. It therefore wouldn't have been a surprise to anyone that when Shah Jahan was taken ill, the two brothers immediately consolidated their armies and went to war. It was April 1658, but the stage had been set for years! The Battle of Dharmat was in fact, a strategically critical battle since it was this battle that would go on to determine the future of the entire subcontinent for years to come. The consolidated armies of Dara Shikoh and Jaswant Singh Rathore of Marwar were pitted against Aurangzeb's mighty forces of heavy cavalry, artillery and muskets. Of course, there could have been plenty of tactics employed to gain the upper hand, but Jaswant Singh was a Rajput, and never in his wildest dreams could he have done anything that did not befit the integrity of the Rajputs. Besides, even though the Rajputs were a military race, Jaswant Singh was a man of letters, a writer, a distinguished intellectual. Perhaps he did not possess the same thirst for blood or the desperation to kill as his much mightier rival. Jaswant Singh though did fight valiantly throughout, his own wounds not deterring him from providing courage to his men. It was only in the end, when defeat was inevitable, that he retreated.

It had turned out to be a hard, bloody battle for everyone and when he saw the condition of the enemy as well as his own men, Aurangzeb decided not to pursue, declaring that he had spared human life as an offering to God. He was however not very merciful toward his brother and father in the aftermath of the battle. Having emerged victorious in a war which had decided the fate of them all, he made complete use of his position, sentenced the brother he hated to a terrible death, and seized the throne from his father. Even the oldest sister, Jahanara, was not spared. Her candid support for her older brother had not gone down well. She got caught in the crossfire and was subsequently removed from her position of *Padshah Begum*. However, when she was sent off to Agra to take care of her imprisoned father, she went gladly, for she was far too faithful to him to abandon him in his hour of need.

There had been many succession battles in the history of the Mughal empire, but the one between Shah Jahan's sons had proved to be the bloodiest of them all. The shocked onlookers who watched in silence were horrified at the atrocities being committed, but ultimately, even they had to accept that a paradigm shift in power was inevitable. Aurangzeb was the new emperor and the mighty Takht Murassa now belonged to him. His coronation was held in Sheesh Mahal at Aizzabad Bagh in Delhi. And it was then that he chose his imperial title. The title was actually in memory of an inscription on the sword his father had given him after the Battle of Samugarh. Alamgir. Conqueror of the world.[8]

As soon as he acceded the throne, Aurangzeb set in motion structured plans to attain his goals of expansion and consolidation. He was of an innately acquisitive nature, and his greed seemed to precede most of his decisions.[9] He adopted a three-pronged strategy of 'defeat, reconcile and place' and this worked very well for him. Realizing the importance of focusing on administrative and military matters, he concentrated on strengthening his prowess in these areas.

Not prepared to allow anything to get in the way of his imperial ambitions, he diligently kept away from what he believed were the 'vices' that several of his antecedents had indulged in. The mysticism of Sufism did not attract him, and he strictly followed the teachings of the more austere form of Sunni Islam. He made it clear that he was not interested in the fine arts though paradoxically, he was a talented veena player himself[10] and the largest number of Persian works on Indian classical music were written during his reign. Also, strangely, despite his staunch religious beliefs and strict adherence to the teachings of Islam, Aurangzeb's court had more Hindu, particularly Rajput administrators than even that of his great grandfather Akbar, who was known to be the most liberal and tolerant Mughal emperor. Personality contradictions notwithstanding, Aurangzeb's ultimate goal was consistent and constant. Every ounce, every iota of his energy and attention was fixed on this one aim, and that was to consolidate the entire sub-continent under his own rule. He was brutal about his ambition from the very start, and his idea of justice was equally harsh. For instance, capital punishment for state enemies was the law of his land, and he soon came to be recognized as one of the most feared rulers the kingdom had known.

While there might have been several policies and strategies that Aurangzeb adopted to further his goal, there was one that had been passed down the generations, from the time of his great grandfather Akbar's reign. Akbar, who had been a wise and ambitious ruler had understood that the Rajputs were a powerful and influential race and working with them would be a prudent decision for his own kingdom.[11] And even though 'The Rajput Policy' as it came to be called, was a combination of diplomacy and aggression, it adopted more of the former rather than the latter.

There were many Rajput rulers who readily cooperated with the Mughals, making consolidation of Mughal power easier. One of the most popular means to achieve this was matrimonial alliances. An age-old practice, matrimonial alliances between the Rajputs and the Mughals were undoubtedly, a stepping stone to military agreements. In several cases, the Rajputs also benefited greatly from such alliances as was the case with the Kachchawaha family. Raja Bhar Mal had been under threat by both the Rana of Mewar and the Mughals. The Kachchawahas had no military strength, but it was the matrimonial alliance with Akbar that gave them a prominent place in the Mughal court.[12] Akbar, in fact, had been known to have extensively used and even advanced this policy and had organized close to forty such marriages for himself, his sons and his grandsons, of which around seventeen had been with the Rajputs. With these Rajput women entering the Mughal harem, the cultural, social and political fabric of the empire changed drastically.[13] Several of the Rajput wives were the chief consorts to their Mughal kings and went on to become the mothers and grandmothers of the future rulers, thus further solidifying the relationship between the two.

It was therefore clear that matrimony was one of the primary routes used to expand, consolidate and control. There were other means also, of course, by which a proposition of friendship and cooperation was offered and accepted. There were however, some exceptions to this as there are to everything. These were the valiant Rajput rulers who did not believe in relinquishing control of their kingdoms and their people to the Mughals. Maharana Raj Singh of Mewar, was one of them.

Raj Singh was no stranger to Aurangzeb. They had a history which went back many years to the time when their fathers had reigned. Raj Singh's father, Rana Jagat Singh, had built a wall around Chittor fort. This had angered Shah Jahan, who felt that Jagat Singh had broken the treaty that his father had made with Amar Singh. Consequently,

Shah Jahan sent his grand vizier, Sadullah Khan, to invade Chittor, and the young Raj Singh personally witnessed the humiliation that was meted out to his father. Jagat Singh was coerced into not only demolishing the wall that had been built but also apologizing to the Mughal emperor in full public view. This angered the son, and he swore revenge, finally getting his chance when Shah Jahan was taken ill in 1657. On the day of Dussehra, the Rajput warrior marched into Kairabad with his army and imposed taxes on the Mughal dominions of Mandal, Pur, Banera and Shahpur. This was also the time when Aurangzeb had opposed his father and brother and seized control of the Mughal throne. Taking his chance, he initiated negotiations with Raj Singh and agreed to give him the territories of Badnaur, Mandalgarh, Dungarpur, Banswara, Basabar and Gyaspur. Naturally, the rulers of these states were not happy with the arrangement, though this did clearly establish Mewar's dominion in the region. Thereafter, there were several instances when the association between the Rana and Aurangzeb went through ups and downs, though neither of them was aware that it would only be in the year 1660 when a monumental event would occur, one that would lead to a battle between two of the greatest military rulers of the time, a battle that would later be remembered by all who would witness it.

CHAPTER 3

The journey from Kishengarh to Delhi was a long one. That meant that the old woman had plenty of time to think over her options. Nirmal's necklace was safely tucked into the folds of her thick shawl, and it felt smooth to her callused hands as she fingered it now and then.

"How easily she removed it from her neck and handed it over to me," the old crone murmured to herself. "But I suppose she must be owning several like this one. It is no wonder that these people are so proud."

Surreptitiously, she ran her hand over the necklace again, savouring the velvety smoothness of the pearls, the sleekness of each ruby and polki rosette. Needless to say, she had never owned anything so valuable though that did not mean that she didn't know the worth of a necklace like this. But was it worthy enough, precious enough, to buy her silence on a matter of such great importance? She knew she had made a solemn promise to Nirmal who had also profusely expressed her regret for the transgression, but shouldn't it have been the Rajkumari who should have apologized? Instead, she had well known what she was doing and had remained as unrepentant as ever. The old woman cringed as she remembered the disdain on the princess's face when she had thrown Alamgir's painting to the ground, followed by the satisfied arrogance with which she had crushed it under the sole of her shoe. "Tsk, tsk! So insolent, so disgraceful!" she said to herself now, shaking her head. "To show such disrespect! Really, she ought to have known better. Reckless actions like these must have consequences."

Her mind made up, she then sat back in the bullock cart to enjoy the last of the journey. The previous *kosminar*[14] had indicated that Shahjahanabad was now not far, but she didn't need a kosminar to tell her that. She'd travelled this route innumerable times, though the first sights and sounds of this walled city built by Shah Jahan, were always fascinating to witness. After all, it was Shahjahanabad that was the official seat of the Mughal government as well as the hub of all cultural and religious activity. With several gates that connected it with its neighbouring region and a ten-kilometre long well that secured it, the city was famous for its bustling *bazaars*, grand mosques and glittering palaces. The Jama Masjid or Masjid-i-Jahan-numa, as it had been named by its creator, occupied pride-of-place. Directly across the mosque was the Lal Qila, the official residence of the Mughal emperors. At this late afternoon hour, the red sandstone and white marble gleamed in the sun as the water from the surrounding moats lapped lazily around the fort walls. Like the Jama Masjid, the fort had also been built by Shah Jahan, with a domination of red and white, the emperor's favourite colours. The grandeur and beauty of the fort could perhaps best be summarized in a couplet inscribed in the Diwan-i-Khas, or hall of private audiences where the emperor received his courtiers and state guests. The couplet in Urdu said,

Agar fardos ba rue Zamin ast
Hamin ast a hamin ast a hamin ast.

Translated into English, it meant, 'If paradise be on the face of the earth, it is this, even this, it is this.'[15]

To the north of the Diwan-i-Khas was located another spectacular attraction that left most visitors awestruck. The Hammam-e-Lal Qila. This was the famed Turkish bath consisting of three domed apartments that were separated by marble corridors. The hammam with its fragrant rose water, colourful inlaid *pietra dura* floral designs made of white marble, and glass skylight that reflected the stars on a clear night, served as a bathing area for the emperor and the royal family. Then, there was the Nahr-i-Bishisht, or stream of paradise. This was the waterway which ran through the Lal Quila, providing a steady supply of water as well as performing the work of a cooling source. It also effectively connected the zenana palaces, which were as astounding in their splendour as the rest of the fort. The archways, the lotus-shaped fountain which was the centrepiece, the flower gardens, the gilded ceilings decorated with intricate mirror work, the carved walls. The *zenana mahal shahi* was the palace constructed by Shah Jahan for his beloved wife, though it was not her, but her daughter Jahanara, who used to live there. Now, since her brother's coronation, she lived in Agra, caring for her ailing, imprisoned father. A short walk away from the shahi mahal was Rang Mahal. Here, the royal ladies of the harem would relax during the day and indulge in music and dance in the evenings. There was a *tehkhana* under the mahal where the ladies could escape on particularly hot days. Of course, the most striking feature of this 'palace of colours' was the mirror work. So magnificent was it that the palace would sometimes also be called Sheesh Mahal, and whenever there was a dance performance there, each dancer would create dozens of reflections, as though hundreds of dancers were performing. It was hardly surprising then that visitors could never quite stop marvelling at the sheer opulence of it all.

The old woman, though, wasted no time in admiring the beauty of the palaces. Instead, once the purpose of the visit had been explained and the necessary permissions granted, she headed straight toward the private chambers of Zeb-un-Nissa, the eldest child of the emperor and his late wife, Dilras Banu Begum.

Born on 15th February 1638, exactly nine months after her parents' marriage, Zeb-un-Nissa was an astutely intelligent young woman, with a mastery over subjects like mathematics, philosophy, astronomy, history, theology and literature. She, in fact, had a natural keenness for literature and poetry and had thoroughly memorized every verse of the Quran and become a *hafiza* at the very young age of seven, setting her apart from all the other women of the kingdom. Her overjoyed father had celebrated this achievement with a grand feast followed by a declaration of a two-day holiday in her honour.[16] He had also proudly presented the young Princess with 30,000 precious gold coins, had rewarded her teacher, Hafiza Mariam, with an additional 30,000 coins and then had promptly distributed the exact same amount among the poor.

Thereafter, the young Princess was tutored by Mohammad Saeed Ashraf Mazandarani, a Persian poet, for her further studies. Revered across the land for her intellectual accomplishments, Zeb-un-Nissa also had a naturally defiant streak in her. That actually wasn't surprising since an astute woman like her was obviously much too sharp to be easily restrained. Despite her rebellious nature though, Zeb was her father's undisputed favourite child,[17] a fact that was known to everyone in the kingdom.

Now as the old woman was led to the young princess's private chambers, she couldn't help thinking back to the scene that had unfolded in front of her eyes, all those miles away in Kishengarh. It had been so shocking, almost unbelievable. The walk from the entrance of the zenana palace to Zeb's chambers took time, but the old woman did not need to mull over her decision anymore. She naturally understood the enormity of the choice she was making, realized the repercussions which couldn't be denied. But then, Alamgir was the emperor, and she had to establish her loyalty toward him. Besides, she didn't want to imagine what would happen to her if he ever became aware of the incident through another source. It was a possibility, after all, there had been many who had witnessed it. Yes, it was certainly in her interest to be the bearer of the news, rather than a victim of the outcome. And who better than Zeb-un-Nissa to help carry out the task? Everyone knew how dear she was to her father and that it was she, who held the most powerful influence on the mighty emperor.[18]

Zeb-un-Nissa was just concluding her daily beauty routine[19] when the old woman was led into her chambers. Tall and slim, the young princess had a creamy complexion, dark, expressive eyes and two beauty spots on her left cheek which were a distinguishing feature. Now, she was sitting in front of a gilded, oval mirror, surrounded by three of her favourite ladies-in-waiting. One of them was drying her thick, dark hair that was still damp from her bath, while another one gently massaged her smooth arms with rose oil. The fragrance of the aromatic oil wafted through the room and the old woman couldn't stop herself from letting out an appreciative sigh. Zeb looked up from the mirror. She saw the hunched-up woman at the door and raised her eyebrows enquiringly at the maid who had escorted her in.

"I understand permission was sought to see me about a rather critical matter. I do not believe I know this woman though. Who is she?"

The woman bowed low. "May I explain my presence in your chambers this afternoon, Your Highness?"

Zeb shrugged. "Unless you would prefer to be thrown into the dungeons for wasting my precious time. This had better be important."

"Have faith, Your Highness. It is important, very important indeed." She cleared her throat. "Earlier this week, I had gone to Kishengarh to sell paintings. It was there that I met Rajkumari Charumati. You may have heard about her. She is known far and wide for her spectacular beauty."

"Yes, I have heard of her." Zeb-un-Nissa shrugged. "I do not, however, believe that you have come here with the sole purpose of regaling me with stories about Charumati's beauty."

"Of course not, Your Highness. Believe me, you will thank me after you hear what I am now about to tell you." The woman took a deep breath and continued. "The Rajkumari was in the zenana courtyard with her friends when I arrived there with my stack of paintings. I asked if she would like to see a few paintings, and she readily agreed. We had all gathered around the marble fountain in the centre of the courtyard. I started showing the paintings to her one by one and...."

The woman spoke slowly, deliberately, stressing on each little detail. Zeb's bored expression soon gave way to a curious interest when the woman started narrating the part about how she had pulled out Alamgir's painting from her stack and shown it to Charumati.

"Did she buy it?" Zeb's eyes narrowed.

The old crone sighed. "Yes, she bought it. Though it was what she did afterward that has really compelled me to come to your doorstep."

"Do not mince words, woman!" One of the oldest *khwajasaras* in the harem interrupted sharply.

The edginess in the *khwaja's* tone was enough to snap the woman out of her tardiness. She realized this was not the time to beat around the bush for effect. "She smashed the painting into a million smithereens, Your Highness. Flung it to the ground and then crushed it under the sole of her bejewelled shoe. Then she went on to curse the emperor, wishing that he meets a similar fate as the painting."

There was a collective gasp of horror from the group of women.

"Ya Allah, ya Allah!"

"Aisi gustakhi!"

"Itna guroor!"

Only the Princess remained silent, her eyes closed, brows furrowed. Her long fingertips tapped the counter of her dressing table. The exclaiming women quietened, their shocked whispers giving way to an expectant hush as they waited for their Princess to react to this news.

Several moments passed and then, finally, Zeb opened her eyes. At first her expression might have seemed impassive, but the old woman who was nearest to her didn't miss the fire in her eyes, nor the quick intake of breath as though the inevitable had been decided. Even as she watched her, the woman knew that this was a significant moment, for it was at this moment that Charumati's fate had been sealed. She was going to be appropriately punished for her blasphemy.

Zeb-un-Nissa turned to the woman. "Thank you for the information. I will see to things now."

The woman clutched her hands to her chest and bowed low. "Please do not thank me, Princess. It was my duty to inform you. I am blessed to have been given an opportunity to express my loyalty to the great emperor."

"Loyalty should always be given its due worth. You shall be well rewarded." Raising her left hand, she indicated to one of her maids. "Escort the woman to the resting room and please take care of her."

The woman beamed all over her wrinkled old face. "*Shukriya*, my Princess. It is my honour to be of service to you and your mighty father. Long live the emperor Alamgir! May he always reign supreme and may his kingdom prosper."

Zeb-un-Nissa smiled at the woman and then the maid led her out of the princess's chambers. Within seconds of her leaving, Zeb dismissed everyone else. Once they had all exited the room, she walked over to the rosewood desk at the end of her chamber. Seating herself in the cushioned chair, she pulled out a loose sheet of paper and her quill. Dating the paper, she then went on to scribble a verse on it. Her teacher, Ustad Bayas, had been the first one to discover Zeb's talent for poetry[20] and had encouraged her to write after she started reciting it at the very young age of fourteen. Her initial writings were in Arabic but an Arabic scholar who read her writings remarked that the poet of the work was an Indian, though he also admitted that it was astounding to see a foreigner with that kind of perfect command over the language. The remark impacted Zeb, and she switched to writing in Persian, her mother tongue. Now poetry came naturally to her. In fact, such was her passion for this Sufi art form, that she often spent her nights in a trance-like poetic stupor. Some were even convinced that she had inherited her love for the Sufi faith from her uncle Dara Shikoh and aunt Jahanara. Others believed that she had been influenced by them. Her father's disapproval of the Sufi faith and all that it stood for, had compelled her to write under the pen name '*Makhfi*'[21] which meant 'the hidden one' in Persian.[22] Unbeknownst to her father, she often attended underground poetic *mehfils*, those secret literary gatherings which were a unique feature in the court of Aurangzeb.[23] Other emperors before him had patronized, even participated themselves in this sublime art form. Akbar was known to have created a grand library of over 24,000 manuscripts during his reign. In the court of Aurangzeb though, poetry was not celebrated. Zeb however, even if she had tried, could not have wrenched herself away from it. Had the famed thirteenth century Persian poet, Jalāl al-Dīn Muhammad Rūmī, not said, '*Be kind to your sleeping heart. Take it out into the vast fields of light and let it breathe.*' And poetry was her heart. How could she not allow it to breathe?

Zeb finished the verse and put the quill down. Joy, rage, disappointment, love, the occasion might be any, poetry was the only outlet she had to express her innermost thoughts. More than anything, poetry gave her clarity. And clarity was what she needed right now. Her face had a contemplative expression as she massaged her temples with the tips of her fingers. She was her father's favourite child. He had a soft spot for her[24], so much so, that she was often able to use her influence and convince him to pardon people who had offended him. This time though, that was not to be. Charumati had crossed all boundaries. To speak ill of someone as mighty, as powerful as the emperor Alamgir. To wish him to be destroyed, to utter such insults. If she was allowed to get away, her father would surely become a laughingstock! No, no, Charumati needed to be taught a lesson. Besides, an example had to be made out of her, so that never again would anyone dare to utter so much as a word against the emperor.

Zeb glanced at the gold *jaali* clock on the opposite wall. There was still some time for the evening salute in the private audience hall, to be followed by the *Maghrib* prayer. With a grim look, the young Princess rose from her chair and strode out of her chambers. This was by no means, an ordinary occasion. It was going to be monumental in its significance, colossal in the magnitude of its repercussions. After all, it was one Princess deciding the fate of another.

CHAPTER 4

The emperor was getting ready for his appearance in the Diwan-e-Khas when a messenger arrived with the news that his eldest daughter wished to speak with him. Already an imposing figure, the frown further added to his grim expression as he wondered what Zeb wished to see him about. She had been sulking with him since the day before when he had refused her a game of chess. An otherwise austere man, he did sometimes concede to his favourite child's wishes, but he was not as keen on chess, as some of his ancestors had been. Chess had been a widely popular form of entertainment in the Mughal court for centuries. His great grandfather was in fact, known to have played live chess in the courtyard of his palace in Fatehpur Sikri, Agra. The exterior *pachisi* board in the courtyard had been famous for using beautiful women as game pieces.[25] And why only entertainment? Sometimes even international games were organized, involving betting with huge stakes. There had been an instance when Emperor Jehangir's courtier had played a match against a Persian diplomat. The game had gone on for three long days and when the Persian diplomat finally lost, his punishment had been to stand there and bray like a donkey in the open court.

His face lined with disapproval, the emperor shook his head. Utterly distasteful! Besides, *Shatranj* was *haram*. Clearly a form of gambling. Perhaps not an offence as serious as alcohol or opium, but an offence, nevertheless. And as far as offences were concerned, his grandfather, Jehangir, had certainly been a case in point. It was hard to imagine him ever taking a sober breath, if you considered the amount of wine and opium he consumed every day. He had been known to mix his opium in wine.[26] Two and a half grams of opium mixed into six cups of wine. That had been his regular potion.

He suddenly noticed the messenger who was still waiting for a response.

Nodding slightly, he said, "I will see the Princess now for five minutes. Please send her in."

Even as he settled down in his favourite armchair, he hoped his daughter had good reason for wanting to see him right now. It was not a convenient time to indulge in small talk, not that he was ever really interested in that. As everyone was aware, his only interest, his sole aim, the one that constantly drove him, was the expansion and success of this empire.

Aurangzeb pressed his lips together. This empire! Reign after reign, ruler after ruler. And now finally, it belonged to him! The very embodiment of power and might. Of course, each ruler who had occupied the *takht* had known that along with the prestige and power, came the hardest challenges that they would have to face. It had been tough from the time of Babur, the very first Mughal. Yes, it had been a splendid triumph when he had defeated Ibrahim Lodi in the Battle of Panipat, thereby bringing an end to the Delhi Sultanate. Thereafter though, it had been an uphill task. He'd faced both external issues from the Afghans and internal ones from his own men. The intensely hot climate of India, the absence of baked bread, *hamams* and the kind of sexual intercourse they were used to, all contributed in making India feel like a foreign land, one in which they did not want to stay.[27] Then his son Humayun had taken over, only to discover that ruling an empire was not an easy task. He'd had serious administrative problems, disputes with his brother, and with the Afghans. Added to that was the threat from Bahadur Shah which had loomed ominously during his reign. That, of course, had only been the tip of the iceberg. The real danger had been from Sher Shah Suri who had him fleeing for his life almost until the very end. Humayun did eventually return and restored Mughal rule too, but tragically died in an accident the following year.

Then had come his great grandfather. Akbar. He'd been a mere child when he'd inherited the throne. The responsibility had stripped him of his childhood, though he was the one who ultimately managed to consolidate a large part of the subcontinent under Mughal rule. A time had come when he had even thought of himself as a messiah, an embodiment of God himself, ordained to change the world.[28] How much his subjects had revered him! The one thing that had been missing from his life however, was the love of his children. It was almost as though a curse had hung over him, depriving him of the very thing he longed for all his life. Of course, historically most Mughal princes had been raised with the knowledge that one day, they would have to fight their own flesh and blood for the takht. That legacy notwithstanding, the particularly lethal rivalry that had existed between Akbar's sons had been a source of worry for the father all his life. His son Salim had turned into a rebel, only to return to claim the throne later. Salim aka Jehangir. The way he had remained in a stupor of lust and wine all his life, it was not surprising that his chief consort Noor Jahan had been the de facto ruler for the later part of his reign.

And how could he forget his own father? Out of sight, out of mind? Not really. Even though Shah Jahan was still in Agra Fort, imprisoned more than a hundred miles away from Delhi, Aurangzeb often thought about him. "Well, whatever his other faults might be," muttered the emperor to himself now. "One thing is clear as day. The old man must have been mad as a hatter, to favour that fool, Dara. Now look at him! Confined in the four walls of that fort. And there he shall stay until the day he dies!"

"Father?"

Aurangzeb was not one to smile frequently but his usually grim face did often break into one when he saw his favourite daughter. Today however, he could sense her mood even before she had entered his room. Bowing her head as everyone did in front of the emperor, she raised her right hand in the traditional Islamic greeting. Her father nodded and invited her to sit.

"And what brings you here, today of all days, Zeb? I thought I would have to ply you with many, many gold coins this time to make up for refusing you that game of chess."

"Life is but a game of chess, Father," Zeb-un-Nissa lifted her eyes. "Do you know the meaning of the word '*Shah Mat*'? It is a famous term in the game."[29]

There was a brief silence in the room. Then the emperor spoke, his eyes narrowed. "You are much too astute to mince words, Zeb," he said. "Surely you have not come here to discuss the terminology of a chess game."

"Shah Mat. It is a Persian word which means 'The king is frozen'. In other words, he is helpless, powerless, unable to respond."

"And that is why I do not waste my time on a game like chess." Aurangzeb smoothened the slight creases on his *jama*. It was a simple white one, and he wore it with a pair of plain white pajamas. His shawl was white too, a minimal one with barely any adornments. A devout *Sunni*, he preferred white and his penchant for the colour was reflected in his clothes. "The emperor always reigns supreme," he concluded then with a firm nod. "He is never frozen! Never helpless, never powerless!"

"Well, there are some who wish it to happen." Zeb-un-Nissa looked her father straight in the eye. She was one of the few who ever dared to do that. "Surely you have heard of Rajkumari Charumati."

"The Princess of Kishengarh. We recently received a rather extravagant present from her brother, Man Singh. I must say he is a smart man. He knows how to maintain cordial relations."

"Unlike his sister."

"What are you talking about, Zeb?"

"Like you said, I am much too astute to mince words. Nor do you have the time for it, Father."

"No, I do not. If you have anything to say that is of importance, say it at once."

"An old woman came to see me this morning. She had been to Kishengarh where she sold a painting of you to Charumati."

"And she did not pay her? Is that what this is about?" The emperor shrugged. "There are many, many paintings of emperors over the years. In fact, in my opinion, too many and too ostentatious."

It was common knowledge that Aurangzeb did not approve of the excessive royal lifestyle that had been commonly portrayed in art before he took over the throne. He was much more inclined toward favouring less extravagant artwork. He especially patronized Islamic calligraphy.[30]

"People buy paintings all the time," he continued then. "What is so special about this news that it has brought you here at an obviously inconvenient time?"

"Father, I agree that people buy paintings all the time. But they do not buy them to smash them into a thousand smithereens and then crush them under the soles of their feet. Nor has anyone before had the audacity to wish ill upon the emperor, to wish him destroyed, finished!"

Aurangzeb slowly turned his head to look at his daughter. There was a quizzical look on his face, almost as though he couldn't quite believe what he'd just heard.

"I do not think I heard you correctly," said the emperor finally. "Surely, you did not just utter those words."

"You heard me perfectly, Father." Zeb-un-Nissa shook her head. "There have been times when I have tried to intervene in your affairs, even implored you to forgive those who have erred. This time, I shall not do so."

As his oldest and favourite child, Zeb-un-Nissa had enjoyed the respect and regard bestowed on her by her father, despite their very different views. Her intellect and astuteness had also ensured her active participation in matters of the court,[31] and she knew that her father took her advice seriously and often acted upon it. There were several instances when people who would otherwise have been severely punished by the merciless emperor had been let off due to Zeb convincing her father otherwise. Her maternal grandfather Shah Nawaz Khan was a case in point. He hadn't supported Aurangzeb during the war of succession, favouring Dara instead. His punishment had been among the first to be announced when Dara was defeated and Aurangzeb took over the throne. If it hadn't been for his favourite daughter's appeals, the old man would surely have been meted out a befitting punishment for his act of disloyalty. Shah Nawaz Khan of course had been Zeb's grandfather, but there were countless others, noblemen and commoners alike, who had been granted the emperor's forgiveness solely because of his daughter. So much so that Zeb would often go to the extent of pleading with her father to grant pardons.

And she was perhaps the only one he found difficult to refuse. Today though, there seemed to be a tacit agreement between them. Certain offences were not to be pardoned under any circumstances.

"It was wise of you to come to me. It is important to do things at the right time, not to delay crucial decisions. And speaking of time, I do not wish to be late for the evening salute." Rising from his chair, the emperor picked up his shawl and draped it around his shoulder. "Least of all for the Maghrib prayer. After all, punctuality is a sign of keeping promises. And we all know the importance that the Quran places on the keeping of a promise, do we not?"

Zeb-un-Nissa nodded. Her father often quoted the Quran to her, this was nothing out of the ordinary. He had in fact, memorized it to perfection and was a hafiz. He was now also in the process of inscribing and writing several passages himself and had entrusted the task of preparing the manuscript to the best calligrapher in the kingdom.

After seeking his permission to leave, she bowed reverently and then withdrew herself from the room. She didn't know exactly what her father was going to do. Would he imprison the Princess? Order her execution? Declare war on Kishengarh? That tiny kingdom didn't stand a chance against the mighty Mughal army. Charumati's brother had managed to maintain peace until now but was he even aware of the blasphemy that had occurred in his palace? And if there was one thing the emperor would never forgive, it was blasphemy.

Zeb knew that her father was feared and dreaded throughout the empire. However, it was only those, including her, who had been witness to the war of succession, who understood the full extent of Aurangzeb's determination and fury. They were the ones, the beholders of this realization, the spectators to an event so historic, so horrific, that they might never again believe in the mercy of man. A bloody battle that left two brothers dead, the third exiled to Burma and the father in confinement, the war of succession had mercilessly torn Shah Jahan's family apart. Estranged from her grandfather and oldest aunt Jahanara, Zeb had silently watched her uncles and their sons being put to death. No one had been spared, no one forgiven.[32]

The Princess shuddered, recalling the memory. To invite the ire of such an emperor, well, the person had to be completely mad!

"Oh Charumati!" exclaimed Zeb-un-Nissa aloud then. "What were you thinking? What was it that took over your senses at that unfortunate moment? Impulse? Childishness?"

"Pride. Pride, arrogance and bitterness."

Zeb turned. The chief eunuch from the zenana had appeared to escort her back to her chambers.

"Never trust your tongue when your heart is bitter," the eunuch continued as they began walking toward the zenana. "And take every effort to guard your tongue, as it is the strongest cause for your destruction."

"Said the wisest of men, the great polymath, Imam Al-Ghazali," nodded the Princess.

"Well, Charumati did not guard her tongue. And so, her destruction is certain," concluded the eunuch.

Chapter 5

Raja Man Singh was standing on the terrace attached to his private rooms, looking down at the main courtyard with keen interest. Apart from the courtyard, the terrace also offered a stunning view of the adjoining flower gardens and the serene Gundalao lake beyond. Dry and arid in the summer months, the recent abundant showers had transformed the lake into a lush water body that was a sight to behold. The *Raja* often spent several hours on his terrace enjoying the view, particularly in the milder months. Today was a hot day, but that hadn't deterred him. Other than the lake, today there was another attraction that had brought him out onto his terrace. *Talwar baazi.* His favourite sport.

At that moment, two of the most skilled swordsmen were competing in a fierce fight that looked like it could go either way. Kishengarh despite being a small state, could boast of some extremely fine swordsmen, though several of the kingdom's best *talwarbazas* were actually women. But that was hardly surprising. Rajput women had historically been a key part of the battlefield. While their fearlessness had been well documented over the years through stories of how they preserved their honour by means of self-immolation and sacrifice, there were countless examples of the valour they could display in politics as well as in the battlefield.[33] Tarabai, Karmavati, Jawaharbai, Mirabai, the list was endless. It was often said about Rajput women, that they were made out of fire. Man Singh sighed. Why look far? His own sister was an example. Headstrong, determined, fearless! So much so that he sometimes couldn't help worrying about her. After their father's tragic death, the role of her protector had passed on to him. But Charumati... she had a mind of her own. He knew that she'd never completely forgiven him for the compromise that he'd made with the Mughal emperor Aurangzeb, after their father's death. Her lack of understanding actually baffled him. Couldn't she imagine the destruction, the plundering that would have befallen their tiny kingdom, had he not accepted the terms of the compromise?

Compromises and alliances had been the reality of the Rajput-Mughal relationship for decades. But then, Charumati was hardly a realist. She was an idealist, a romantic. She lived in her own world, a world of black and white. And yes, Man Singh had to admit, at least to himself, that in many ways, she was braver than him.

So lost was he in his own thoughts that he didn't realize when the game was concluded and the winner declared. Even as the victor lifted his sword triumphantly and the onlookers cheered for him, Man Singh smiled to himself. How often had he and Charu faced each other in a game of talwar baazi in this same courtyard? Dressed in identical white kurtas and churidars, with the end of a white turban draped across the face, all the contenders looked the same and spectators would often not be able to guess whether it was a man or a woman wielding the sword. Charu, despite being so much slighter than her brother, was a skilled swordswoman but then talwar bazi was a game of tactical strategy rather than strength. Skill, concentration and precision were the deciding factors, and she seemed to have those in abundance. She was however, very emotional and often given to taking reckless decisions. That could just be youth, but their late father had often warned her that emotion which led to impulsiveness often became one's downfall. Now Charu was older and with any luck, wiser. Even as he considered it, Man Singh couldn't help wondering whether it was time to start thinking about his sister's betrothal. With her beauty, charm and intelligence, Charu would attract the best of Rajput suiters though Man Singh was aware of his sister's ardent admiration for Rana Raj Singh. She hadn't spoken to him about it, but he knew her well.

"*Hukum?*"

Man Singh turned. A *darbaan* stood at the door. The next pair of talwarbaazas were getting ready to face each other off in the courtyard. With a regretful last glance at them, Man Singh walked back into the room and waved the darbaan in.

"*Ghani Khamma,* Hukum. There is a messenger waiting to see you. He has come from the durbar of Emperor Aurangzeb."

Man Singh nodded. The emperor must have received the present he'd sent him and undoubtedly wished to thank him for his generosity. Perhaps the messenger had even brought him an invitation to visit the Diwan-e-Khaas. It had been a while since he'd met the emperor.

"Please take care of him," Man Singh instructed the darbaan. "He has come from the emperor's court and is our honoured guest. I will meet him presently."

"Ji Hukum," the darbaan bowed and retreated.

An hour later, the Raja met the messenger in his private durbar. Dressed in a black kurta and churidar with a black turban wound about the head, the end of its drape hanging loose down the shoulder, the bearded messenger was as poker faced as ever. His expression, just like his outfit, seemed to be completely devoid of colour. Man Singh on the other hand, had changed into an elaborate gold achkan, churidar, pagadi and kamarbandh. Only six of his most trusted ministers were present at the time, other than the fan bearer on his right side. After the messenger had greeted him, Man Singh asked him to read out the *shahi farmaan*. Even as the messenger undid the scroll, Man Singh got a sudden feeling that this was not an invitation to visit. The messenger's demeanour gave nothing away, but Man Singh couldn't help the sense of premonition that strangely seemed to take over his senses. It was a feeling akin to knowing that something ominous was about to happen.

"The Mughal emperor, Abu'l Muzaffar Muhi-ud-Din Muhammad Aurangzeb Alamgir, sends you his fondest greetings. With a wish to bring your kingdom under his protection, and to further the friendship that exists between Shahjahanabad and Kishengarh, he sends a marriage proposal for your sister, Princess Charumati. Your acceptance of this proposal will be proof of your loyalty to the emperor and will lead to a solidifying of the alliance between our kingdoms."

The first thought that came to the shocked Man Singh's mind was that he had inherited the throne far too early. After Roop Singh's untimely death, there were many things that his young, inexperienced son had had to learn and grasp for the good of his small kingdom, but never before had he felt as trapped, as alarmed as he did at that moment. In normal circumstances, receiving a marriage proposal for a daughter or a sister was an occasion to be celebrated. Charu was not yet betrothed to anyone, but the decision to accept a proposal or not was always one that was taken after careful consideration. This proposal, however, had come from none other than Aurangzeb! Where was the choice? What was the option? If anything, this was certainly not a proposal, whatever anyone chose to call it. While matrimonial alliances between the Mughals and the Rajputs had been ongoing for centuries, Man Singh couldn't shake off the feeling that there was something inexplicably disturbing about this particular scenario. And Charu... a Mughal bride? Knowing his sister as well as he did, Man Singh was certain that she would never agree to this. But rejecting a proposal from Aurangzeb? Even the thought was inexcusable.

Man Singh tried to steady the beating of his heart. With a calmness that he did not feel, he folded his hands and smiled at the messenger.

"Please thank the emperor on our behalf. It is indeed an honour to receive this proposal from him. We are humbled and grateful. Rest assured; the emperor will receive a response from us at the earliest."

If the messenger was surprised at not receiving an affirmative response right then, he did not show it. Nodding slightly, he thanked the Raja and then allowed himself to be escorted to the lavish lunch that was waiting for him. Visitors to the palace were always treated with respect and unfailingly received the warm hospitality that the Rajputs were famous for. And a guest from the emperor's durbar was an honoured one indeed. Food, though, was the furthest thing from Man Singh's mind even as he shook his head and wiped the beads of perspiration that had gathered at his temples. He looked around at the worried faces of his closest, most faithful ministers and knew that the same questions were running through their minds, too. Would he accept this proposal, even if it meant going against Charumati's wishes? Or would he reject it and invite the wrath of the mighty Aurangzeb, a wrath that would surely wipe out every trace of the tiny kingdom of Kishengarh?

"*Ghor sankat!*" One of his oldest ministers finally broke the silence in the room. "Princess Charumati will never agree to this alliance. She cannot bear the sight of the emperor. She would much rather end her life."

The minister who had spoken had served in Roop Singh's court for decades and had seen both children growing up. He had known Charumati since she was a little girl.

"Yes, she will never agree to be a Mughal bride," agreed another minister. "Though I dare not even imagine what will befall Kishengarh when the emperor gets to know."

"Why are we making a mountain out of a molehill?" remarked a third minister. "There have been many successful marriage alliances between the Mughals and the Rajputs. Akbar and Jodha Bai, for instance."

"Pardon me for saying this, but do you not see any difference between Akbar and his great grandson?"

The first minister looked enraged. "As far as I know it, none other than the present emperor, succeeded the throne in the manner that he did. His father still alive and imprisoned, his older brother humiliated, paraded in tattered clothes and chains all over Delhi before being executed![34] Why, he even exhibited his headless body, I personally witnessed the open outcry that reverberated around the city. That monster Jiwan Khan who cunningly captured Dara, was pelted with so much dirt and filth that he had to flee the streets, barely saving his own life![35] It is no wonder that Aurangzeb's own father used to routinely call him 'a white serpent'. The epithet suits him perfectly."

"Say what you want but as far as the succession to the throne is concerned, everyone knows that it is a matter of survival of the fittest." The third minister spoke calmly. "Dara with his placid nature and artistic outlook did not stand a chance. Aurangzeb, on the other hand, has a reputation of being ruthless on the battlefield."

"That is my primary concern," Man Singh folded his hands and addressed his ministers. He simply could not take any decisions with half a dozen pairs of anxious eyes staring at him. "I understand and appreciate what each one of you has said. I also know that while your views and judgements might be different, all of you have one thing in common. Concern for Kishengarh. Now if you will allow me, I must think over this very carefully. *Ekant*."

Once the ministers had dispersed, the Raja returned to his rooms. There were usually two motives for a matrimonial proposal being sent. Military was one. If at all Aurangzeb was looking for a military alliance, then Kishengarh was small fry compared to some of the other kingdoms in the region. Why would he set his sights on their tiny state? On the other hand, undeniably, Charu was a very charming young woman and tales about her mesmerizing beauty had indeed spread far and wide. It was likely that the emperor had heard about her and become smitten. That was most certainly the greater possibility.

Despite that, there was something unusual about this particular proposal. Almost as though it had appeared out of thin air. No warning, no indication at all. Something was amiss. Something that he was not aware of.

Man Singh walked to the door with rapid strides. The darbaan was a tall, hefty, moustached man in a red and yellow uniform. He became alert as soon as he saw the Raja approaching.

"Ask Princess Charumati to come and see me right now. Tell her it is an urgent matter, and she absolutely must not delay."

"Ji Hukum!" With a brisk bow, the darbaan disappeared down the long corridor. Man Singh turned and walked back into the room. His whole body ached with sudden exhaustion, but he knew that could just be the tension of the past couple of hours. With a sigh, he lowered himself into his favourite ivory inlaid armchair, the one with the alternating ivory and horn geometrical pattern and matching ottoman. The matter was critical, but his nerves were frayed, his head throbbing. It was a ten-minute walk from the zenana. Leaning back, Man Singh stretched his legs out, his feet resting on the ottoman, and closed his eyes.

"Bhai sa?"

It seemed as though he had only just dozed off when he was awakened from his slumber by the sound of his sister's voice. Even as he opened his eyes, he could smell the fragrance of the *chandan* oil she always used in her bath water. Despite his frazzled state of mind, the perfume had a soothing effect on him. Man Singh swung his legs down from the ottoman and pulled himself to a sitting position. He indicated to his sister to take one of the carved *pida* chairs opposite him and she made a face.

"Bhai sa! This is why I dislike meeting you here. Why do you not change the seating arrangement in this room?"

Man Singh laughed, temporarily forgetting the dilemma at hand. "Why? What is wrong with the seating arrangement here? I think it is very comfortable."

Charu looked pointedly at her brother's armchair and shook her head. "Of course it is. For you. For the rest of us...." The young Princess rolled her eyes and then with exaggerated resignation, lowered herself into the pida chair. Man Singh watched as she fidgeted with her lehenga and odhni, trying to adjust them with her delicate fingers. Lips pursed together, there was a petulant look on her face as she struggled with the skirt of the lehenga that had gathered in a heap around her feet due to the low chair. It was evident she was not happy with the chair, and she made no effort to conceal her discomfort. But Charu was like that. If she did not like something, small or big, she had no qualms about expressing how she felt. Man Singh sighed and waited for her to finish.

Charu looked up at last. Even as she faced her brother, she instantly noticed his worried expression. "What is it, Bhai sa? You look distressed. Is everything all right?"

"No everything is not all right, Charu." Man Singh did not want to waste any more time. The messenger must have departed for

Shahjahanabad by now and every second was precious. "A messenger came to see me today. He was from the durbar of the Mughal emperor Aurangzeb."

Charu's expression became quizzical for a moment, as though she couldn't understand why her brother was telling her this. Messengers came from all over to meet the king and it certainly wasn't the first time that one had visited from Shahjahanabad. And then suddenly, almost like the lifting of a curtain, a look of comprehension dawned on her face. Man Singh watched her carefully as her left hand moved to clutch the end of her odhni. Even as she twisted it round and round, he couldn't help but sense that she seemed nervous, anxious. He could have waited for her to explain her unease, but the situation was far too urgent.

"I get the sense that you know more about this than I do. I am usually always aware of the goings on in my kingdom, but with you Charu, I can never be sure. Please tell me everything you know. As you can well imagine, this is hardly a trivial issue."

Charumati continued to fiddle with the odhni. There had been many difficult moments that her brother and she had shared over the years, most of all when the news about their father's untimely passing had come. The siblings had always been close and Roop Singh's death had brought them closer still. The loving relationship they shared had allowed them to lean on each other for support, to be completely honest with each other. This was the first time she found herself faltering, hesitating in front of her brother. How could she tell him the truth about what had happened in the courtyard that day? He would be horrified, furious!

"Stop that, Charu."

Man Singh's voice had suddenly taken on a harsher tone as he indicated to his sister to stop fidgeting. "I find your demeanour very discomfiting. Has anything happened that I am not aware of?"

"What did the messenger say?" Charu released the odhni and lifted her eyes to meet her brother's gaze.

"I do not appreciate being asked a question in response to mine. Please tell me everything you know. And keep it brief."

The urgency in Man Singh's voice snapped her to attention. With a beating heart, she told him everything that had happened in the courtyard the day the woman with the paintings had visited. Difficult though it was, she did not leave anything out. Not the harshness of her words, not the shock and distress on the old woman's face, not even the way the sound had reverberated around the open courtyard when she'd thrown the painting to the ground and shattered it into hundreds of minuscule pieces. Man Singh's expression changed from concern to distress and then finally to horrified disbelief as he listened to his sister and the picture became crystal clear in his mind. This wasn't just a marriage proposal. This was a means to teach Charu a lesson. A means to make an example out of her so that nobody, anytime, anywhere, would ever again dare to utter a word against the emperor.

"But Nirmal told me that the old woman swore on her life. She promised that not a word of what had happened would ever leave the safe confines of our palace," Charu looked imploringly at her brother. "Surely, she would not have broken her promise like this. A promise is everything. A promise is sacred."

"For a Rajput, yes. A Rajput will give up his life to keep a promise. Unfortunately for us, the old woman was not a Rajput."

Man Singh shook his head. "Charu, Charu! How many times did Baba warn you to not let your emotions take over your senses? Why did you never heed his advice?"

"I could not help it, Bhai sa! I could not control my disdain, my rage. I almost felt as though she was trying to mock me by showing me that painting. All this would never have happened if she had not pulled it out of the stack."

"There is no point crying over spilt milk now. What is done, is done."

"What will happen now, Bhai sa? Have I endangered Kishengarh in any way? Tell me!"

Man Singh knew that Charu's first thoughts were for Kishengarh and its people, not for herself. An act of blasphemy like this often led to enmity between two kingdoms and subsequently, the stronger one declared war on the other. Power, honour, pride, revenge, there were so many motivations, so many provocations.

Aurangzeb. Alamgir. Conqueror of the world. Seizer of the world. He had certainly earned the title. Not much time had passed since he became emperor, but he was already the most feared of them all. He was a man who spared no one, not his own flesh and blood, not even his own father. A man whose reputation preceded him. He would never allow anyone to tamper with that reputation, to damage it. And Charumati had done just that. She had scorned him. Insulted him. Cursed him. Now someone would have to pay the price. And that someone would have to either be her, or the people of Kishengarh.

"You ask if you have endangered Kishengarh," Man Singh sighed. "Let me be very honest with you, Charu. If the Mughals declare war on us, their army will annihilate us in no time. We do not stand any chance."

"Is that why the messenger came here to see you, Bhai sa?" There were tears in the young princess's eyes, but she blinked them back resolutely.

"Quite the contrary," Man Singh laughed mirthlessly. "If love is the opposite of war, then quite the contrary, my dear sister."

"Bhai sa, I cannot unravel these mysteries. Please tell me clearly what the messenger said."

Man Singh knew that there would never be an easy way to say this. Charu would have to face the truth. He came straight to the point. "Emperor Aurangzeb has sent a marriage proposal for you, Charu. Of course, the word 'proposal' is merely a word. Aurangzeb never proposes anything, he simply commands, and anyone who does not obey the command has to suffer the consequences. I am afraid that...."

"Bhai sa!" Charumati looked at her brother in horror. "Do not even utter the words. I swear on our father's urn that I will never marry that man. I do not care about what happens. I will never do this, never!"

"I understand that this is an enormous shock to you, Charu," Man Singh tried to appeal to his sister to think clearly. "But this is not the first time a proposal has been sent for a marriage alliance between the Rajputs and the Mughals. I can give you many examples of very successful marriages between the two."

"And I can give you many examples of valiant, honourable Rajputs who never entered into any alliances like this," Charumati's voice shook with rage. "The Sisodias of Mewar for instance. Maharana Pratap was on his death bed when he took a vow from his son Amar Singh that he would never ally with the Mughals. Even today they stand by the honour of their ancestors.[36] Look at Rana Raj Singh! Did Aurangzeb not ask him to send contingents for help during the war of succession with his brothers? Raj Singh refused. Not once but multiple times. He has proven to be a formidable enemy for the emperor, and everyone knows it."

Man Singh shook his head sadly. "And you see no difference between Raj Singh's mighty army and our small kingdom? You see no difference between Mewar and Kishengarh? I cannot help but marvel at your naivete, Charu."

"I might be naïve, Bhai sa. But I do understand one thing. If like Mewar, the other Rajput kingdoms had also stuck together, we would have been a force to reckon with. Nobody would have dared to set eyes on our land or our people.[37] Do you not agree?"

Man Singh stared at his sister. Why did she always ask such questions? Questions to which he had no answers, yet questions that he himself wondered at sometimes. After all, the Rajputs were a common race, with common traditions, customs, language. Why then had they been unable to put up a united front against a common adversary? Perhaps his sister was right. This constant internal battling for power had cost them all dearly.[38]

Charumati's fury at seeing her brother so helpless suddenly turned to desperation. Wringing her delicate hands together, she wailed. "Please, Bhai sa! This cannot be my destiny. It cannot. There has to be a way out. There has to be!"

"Charu please! Try to look at the bright side."

"What bright side?" Charumati looked at Man Singh in bewilderment. "There is no bright side."

"Everyone knows that Mughal emperors and the princes of the royal blood only marry within ruling families. Even ordinary nobles are never considered.[39] This may anger you, but there are many who would consider this proposal a matter of prestige and honour."

Charumati stared at her brother with such loathing that he ultimately had no choice but to look away from her scathing gaze. It was the second time in their entire lives that she had looked at him that way. The first time had been years ago when they had been just children. He had broken the puppet groom in her *kathputli* set and she had flown at him, trying to claw at his face in anger. Laughing, he had held her hands and at their father's insistence, had solemnly committed that he would replace the groom. He'd forgotten to do it and she hadn't spoken to him for weeks afterward. That had been the only time. And now this. This time, though, he had no words that could offer any comfort to his sister. Ironically, this time, he actually felt like a mere puppet himself.

Hukum! It was what everyone called him, did they not? They followed his every order, obeyed his smallest instruction. Right now, even the title felt like a mockery.

Mustering all the courage he could, Man Singh lifted his head.

"Charu," he looked straight into his sister's eyes. "I will be writing to the emperor as soon as possible, accepting his proposal. If it makes you feel any better, let me tell you that you are not the first to have to sacrifice for the sake of her people. Nor will you be the last. Please do not fight this. Accept your fate."

Charumati fell to the floor, beating her chest with grief and frustration. So piteous were her cries that Man Singh was sure they would have melted the most austere of hearts. But he was a Raja and for him, nothing could ever be greater than his *praja*. His first responsibility was toward them and if he had to sacrifice his family for their good, then be it. He didn't know what their father, the late Raja Roop Singh would have done in his place, but he had taken his decision. Charumati would have to marry Aurangzeb. It was the only way to keep the peace.

CHAPTER 6

Jodhpuri Begum had spent her entire life in a women's zenana. Strictly maintaining purdah and living in a walled, screened portion of the palace hadn't been something she'd questioned. It was that way for all Rajput noblewomen.[40] The zenana was a world of its own, where all the queens, queen mothers, princesses, widows of important generals, *dais*, concubines, co-existed. The women were well versed with literature, art, craft, poetry and music and even went on hunting and polo trips on a regular basis. Weddings were celebrated in a grand manner and festivals like Basant Panchami, Holi, Teej and Diwali provided some respite from their otherwise restrictive lives.

Jodhpuri Begum became Aurangzeb's first Rajput wife when she married him and moved to the Shahi harem in Lal Qila. The first thing she noticed was that unlike the zenana in her palace, here she did not have to observe *ghoonghat* in front of the senior women of the harem[41] and she did inwardly rejoice at that unexpected freedom. At least in the harem, women were free to dress the way they wanted. There was a protocol in the harem of course and the emperor's closest female relatives wielded the maximum power, with the Padshah Begum being the chief authority. The title quite literally meant 'lady emperor' and this coveted position was usually always bestowed upon the first wife of the emperor.

However, in Aurangzeb's harem, it was his sister Roshanara Begum and oldest daughter Zeb-un-Nissa who pulled all the strings. Aurangzeb's oldest wife Dilras Banu Begum had passed away a year before he became emperor. Dilras had been his imperial consort till she died, and that position was never filled by another wife. Of course, other than the indifference of her husband, there was not much for Jodhpuri to complain about. Her life in the harem was a comfortable one and there was no dearth of material luxuries or indulgences.

Jodhpuri looked around at the beautiful suite of rooms that had belonged to her since she'd entered the harem after her marriage to the emperor. The polished marble floors, the tinkling water fountain, the mirrored walls, the plush Persian rugs, the heady fragrance of roses. She thought about her closets, crammed full with the finest muslins, velvets and brocades. The jewellery boxes overflowing with precious stones and pearls. Most people would call her '*khushnaseeb*'.

'*Sone ka pinjra*,' Jodhpuri sighed as she remembered the woman's words. She had been one of Dara's concubines, an extraordinarily beautiful young woman from Kashmir. After Dara's death, she had continued living in the harem. A wonderful dancer, she often entertained the other women, but there was a desolate look in her eyes that always touched Jodhpuri's heart.

"Dancing must make you very happy," Jodhpuri had remarked to her once after a particularly spectacular performance. The young woman had smiled wistfully, her eyes intoxicated with opium.

"Dance when you are broken open," she'd said then. "Dance in your blood. Dance when you are free. Dance until you shatter yourself!" Jodhpuri had looked baffled, and the woman had thrown her head back and laughed.

"So said the wonderful Sufi poet, Jalaluddin Mohammad Rumi![42] You know, Begum Sahiba, when I was a little girl, I used to dance amidst a forest of wild trees. On moonlit nights, the lake would shimmer like a diamond and the perfume of mulberries would fill the air." She'd then paused to look around.

"Yeh toh sone ka pinjra hai. I don't dance here, I simply perform."

"Jodhpuri Begum!"

Snapping out of her thoughts, Jodhpuri turned. Farooq Khan Khwajasara stood before her, his face flushed. He was panting from running fast.

"Is everything okay?" Jodhpuri looked at him in concern. Farooq had entered the harem as a young boy and had spent close to twenty-five years serving Shah Jahan's family. He was the one who had been assigned to her from the very first day, the one who had familiarized her to the ways of the shahi harem. Loyal, astute and sharp, Farooq was usually among the first ones to hear any news that made its way through the doors of the harem.

"Have you heard?" Farooq tilted his head and Jodhpuri smiled.

"No, I have not, but I am sure I will now. What news have you brought?"

Farooq placed his index finger on his chin and stared at Jodhpuri out of heavily kohled eyes. "News travels fast in the harem, Jodhpuri Begum. Then it becomes difficult to separate truth from rumour. You must never underestimate the role of the khwajasaara. As Abul Fazl categorically stated in his *Akbarnama*, the khwajasaara has been the most important link between the harem and the outside world."[43]

"Then you must perform your duty, Farooq. Tell me. What news could be so monumental as to make you lose your breath?"

"Not in front of them," Farooq shifted his eyes toward the pair of parrots that lived in a gilded cage in Jodhpuri's room. "They are such scandalmongers. They will repeat everything to everyone!"

Laughing, Jodhpuri led Farooq into the inner sanctum of her mahal. Her bedroom. Here, it was even quieter, so much so that she could hear every tinkle of the water fountain as it spouted crystal-clear water into the marble bowl below. "Is this private enough?" she raised her eyebrows enquiringly.

Farooq looked around one last time to make sure and then nodded. "I have heard that something blasphemous has happened in Kishengarh. Something that has outraged the pride, the honour of our kingdom. *Shehzaadi* Zeb-un-Nissa received the news and immediately reported it to the emperor."

"Kishengarh? But I thought Raja Man Singh and the emperor were on civil terms with each other."

"It was not the Raja. It was the Rajkumari. Charumati. She apparently smashed a painting of the emperor, crushed it under the sole of her foot and then cursed him repeatedly."

Jodhpuri looked horrified. "She did that?"

"Yes! Can you believe it?"

Jodhpuri shook her head. "I cannot even begin to imagine what the emperor will do now. I suppose he will declare war on that tiny kingdom. It will all be over even before it begins."

"Well, as the founder of this great empire said, 'If you desire to rule and conquer, you do not just fold your hands when things go wrong. You act.' Our emperor has much in common with his great-great-great-grandfather." Farooq Khan lifted both his hands upwards, palms toward his face. "*Ya Allah!* I would not like to be in Charumati's shoes right now."

"Has the emperor made a decision?" Jodhpuri stared at the eunuch.

"Yes. Charumati's destiny has been sealed. The emperor has sent a marriage proposal to Kishengarh."

"A marriage proposal?" Jodhpuri's hand flew to her mouth. "The emperor wishes to marry her?"

"I suppose he wishes to rein her in. Teach her a lesson. And *mashallah*, the Rajkumari is supposed to be very beautiful. That does not hurt, does it?" Farooq giggled nervously. "This marriage will make Charumati the emperor's second Rajput wife, after you. You might welcome the company, though I have heard that women thrive on novelty."

Jodhpuri raised her eyebrows. "Why do you believe you understand women so well, Farooq?"

"Only because we khwajasaras have unhindered access to them. Unlike the poor men," Farooq laughed raucously.

"Has the proposal been received in Kishengarh?"

The question had a note of urgency that instantly made Farooq discard all attempts at levity.

"A messenger was sent. Their answer is awaited," Farooq spread his hands out. "Not that they have a choice. Unless they want to have their small kingdom razed to the ground."

After Farooq had left, Jodhpuri poured herself a glass of rose *sherbet* from the pitcher on her bedside table. Farooq was a compulsive chatterbox and all the talking had made her throat dry. Glass in hand, she settled down on the *diwan* by the *jaali* window. From her vantage point, she could see that the main zenana courtyard was being readied for a dance performance that was going to happen that evening, but she did not plan on attending. She needed to be on her own.

Sone ka pinjra. Somehow, the concubine's words kept coming back to her. There were plenty of women who were happy with the secure, luxurious lives they were leading in the harem, some even more so since they had been rescued from lives of slavery and penury. But there were many who would agree with the concubine. However gilded a cage might be, it was still a cage that imprisoned you, isolated you from the outside world. If it could crush the soul of any free-spirited woman, what would it do to a woman who was being brought there with the sole intention of punishing her for a grave act of blasphemy? No doubt, she would soon wither away and die.

And Charumati. She was young, beautiful, bold. She was brave, too. A true Rajput Princess. Everyone knew how much her father had doted on her before he passed away in that unfortunate incident. Despite having spent her days in the zenana, she had been bestowed with the kind of freedom that most women could not take for granted. Her unrestrained demeanour was evident in the way she had spoken her mind, with no thought, no heed to the repercussions. That, though, had been her mistake. Her transgressions should never have crossed the boundaries of Kishengarh. Now they had made their way to Shahjahanabad and everyone knew that Aurangzeb's capital did not forgive or forget.

Even as she thought about it, an idea gradually started forming in her mind. Farooq was correct in thinking that Kishengarh would be instantly wiped out if push came to shove and they dared to stand up to the mighty Mughal army. But wasn't there someone, anyone, who was brave enough, capable enough to help the princess? From resisting the enemy, to eventually aligning with them, the Rajput states had been divided for many decades now. Several Rajput kingdoms were now allies to the Mughals, Jodhpuri's own kingdom included. On the other hand, there were still some rulers who hadn't given up their efforts to resist and challenge, and had managed to hold on to the sovereignty of their kingdoms. In the latter category, Mewar was the strongest, most able kingdom, with a glorious history of resistance and defiance. From the time of Rana Sanga to Maharana Pratap, rebellion was in their blood. Hadn't Maharana Pratap been on his deathbed when he'd taken a solemn promise from his son that he would never submit to the enemy and would win Chittor back? The current ruler Rana Raj Singh had already demonstrated that he meant to uphold everything that his ancestors stood for. Yes, if there was anyone who could save the Rajkumari from this fate, it was Raj Singh.

Jodhpuri rose and swiftly walked to her writing desk. She was surprised to see how quickly the last few hours had passed. Dusk had fallen and the sky at that moment was a particular hue of deep lavender that always reminded her of warm sunsets over a desert horizon. How gloriously beautiful the sunsets had looked from her bedroom window in her father's palace. Golden sunbeams scattered over rolling sand dunes and somewhere far, a caravan of camels silhouetted against the resplendent palette of colours. Jodhpuri sighed. This was no time for reminiscing. The emperor was not the kind who would sit around waiting for Charumati to accept or reject his proposal. If the acceptance did not come soon, he would get his troops together and set off for Kishengarh. Settling down in the chair, Jodhpuri pulled a sheet of clean parchment paper from the stack on her desk, picked up her quill, and started writing.

By the time she had folded and sealed the letter, the sounds of sarangi, tabla and veena had started flowing in from the courtyard. Some people did say that Aurangzeb was far too austere to really appreciate music or even art, but Jodhpuri knew that her husband was a talented veena player himself.[44] Music had been an integral part of life in the shahi harem, in fact in the entire kingdom, since the time of the first emperor. The Mughals had historically been keen patrons and the tradition of music and dance had continued through the decades. A mesmerizing amalgamation of Persian and Indian compositions, music in the Mughal court was distinctly different from the *Panihari* and *Maand* folk songs that Jodhpuri had grown up on. Now, even as she started tapping her fingers on the ebony desk and her head began swaying in time to the music, Jodhpuri acknowledged to herself that she was slowly but surely growing accustomed to a completely different life.

"Well, hopefully Rajkumari Charumati will not have to," she murmured to herself as she rose from the desk and made a mental note to send the letter the following morning itself. Not a moment could be wasted.

CHAPTER 7

The normally lively women's palace had been unusually quiet since the day that messenger had left. Every morning, the *aarti* was performed, and the *prasad* distributed. After that, all the ladies tried to go about their daily tasks with as much normalcy as possible. The senior ladies planned the menus, the maids busied themselves with their regular chores of cooking, cleaning and washing, the older ladies sewed and played cards. All the time, though, there was a pall that hung heavy in the zenana. A palpable feeling of gloom that was unanimously shared by them all, irrespective of age and status. Only the children played as usual with abandon, oblivious to the dread that everyone else was feeling.

The news had spread like wildfire around the zenana, and within a few hours, everyone knew. Some of the girls who had been present when Charumati had smashed the painting had shaken their heads and exchanged knowing looks as though to say to each other, "This was bound to happen."

Nirmal, though, despite herself expecting the worst, had looked at Charumati with shocked eyes when the Princess related to her, the conversation she had had with her brother.

"*Hai Ram!*" Nirmal had wailed. "That old crone! I should have known that she could not be trusted."

Charu had laughed mirthlessly. "Yes, you never should have given her that heirloom necklace. For how many decades has it been in your family, Nirmal? Such a waste!"

Nirmal stared at her friend. "I cannot believe you are talking about a necklace when your entire life is at stake here."

Charu shrugged. There was something so despondent about the gesture, as though she had already given up hope. Given up the fight without fighting.

After that, she had locked herself up in her room. At first, Nirmal and the other girls had been terrified at finding the door bolted from inside. Charumati was emotional and given to impassioned outbursts, and they were afraid of what she might do. Then, when Nirmal managed to peek into the bedroom through one of the jaali windows, she was relieved to see Charumati lying on the bed, staring up at the ceiling. The ornate gold filigree work on the fourteenth century ceiling was so beautiful that it unfailingly brought a smile to the princess's face, despite the fact that she looked at it every day. Now, she didn't seem to be noticing anything, as she just lay there, staring up vacantly. Later, when Nirmal, accompanied by Charumati's chief *daasi*, returned to tell Charumati that lunch had been served in the dining hall, she responded with a shake of the head. However, she didn't put up a protest when Nirmal quietly asked the daasi to serve the Rajkumari's lunch in her room. Perhaps the fragrance of *gatte ki sabzi, lahsun ki chutney* and *choorma* was too irresistible even for a Princess in distress.

Today, when Nirmal entered the room, the first thing she noticed was that the rose petals in the marble fountain had completely dried out. This was hardly surprising since Charumati had not been allowing anyone to enter her room except to serve food. Like the previous evening, she was lying on her carved acacia bed, staring up at the ceiling. It seemed to have become her habitual position.

"This will not help Charu." Nirmal's silver anklets made a tinkling sound as she walked around the breadth of the bed and sat down next to her friend. "You have to face the truth. And then, you have to either accept or defy. Denial is not a solution."

"I would rather die, Nirmal." Her voice was a whisper, but every word was clear.

"He is not concerned with your life or death." Charumati knew Nirmal was talking about the emperor. Shaking her head, she turned away, as though that could refute the reality of the situation.

Cupping her friend's face in her hands, Nirmal gently turned it back toward her. Charu did not have the luxury to indulge in wallowing. A decision had to be taken urgently. "Try to understand Charu. His aim is to avenge the insult that you meted out to him and to make an example out of you. If he is unable to do so, Kishengarh will have to bear the brunt of his wrath. Our troops will try to defend us, but they will not stand a chance against that mighty army. Civilians will be killed or enslaved, women will have to commit *jauhar* to save their honour, even the children will not be spared."

Charu closed her eyes, allowing the tears to fall. "I will sacrifice myself for the sake of my people, Nirmal. Tell Bhai sa to accept the emperor's proposal. He can satisfy his pride by marrying me. But I swear upon Bhavani Ma, he will not have me."

She opened her clenched palm and showed Nirmal the tiny bottle of poison she was holding. "I will drink this before the *doli* reaches Shahjahanabad. In any case, it is their favourite way to punish, is it not?"

It was a well-known fact that killing by poisoning was an age-old practice among the emperors to punish or silence any kind of rebellion, enmity, disloyalty or blasphemy. Poust or a concoction of raw opium would be served to those suspected of treachery. Poisoned *khilats* were another preferred choice, those beautiful robes of honour that would be impregnated with lethal poisons so that the wearer would die an excruciatingly painful death.[45] Birthdays, coronations, festivals, elevation into or within the mansabdari system, there were innumerable occasions when this lethal weapon could be used to silence an enemy or traitor.

"We can think of my wedding *poshak* as a poisoned khilat." Charumati shrugged. "Do not fret for me, Nirmal. Now that I have made my decision, I am at peace. There was never any other alternative after all."

"I never knew you to give up so easily, Charu." Nirmal looked at her friend in surprise and then got up and walked to the window of the room. She waved a hand in the general direction of the fort's exterior. "We all remember how and why your father built this fort, do we not?"

Charu stared at her friend, not comprehending the sudden change of subject. Then she nodded, a wistful expression on her beautiful face. "How can I not remember?" she said. "He must have told me that story a hundred times. He saw a sheep protecting her lambs from a vicious pack of wolves. That is why he built this fort. To protect his empire. See how tall the gates, roofs and walls are? That was all done on purpose. To keep the kingdom as secure as possible."

"He was a remarkable ruler, Charu. And you are his daughter. How can you think of giving up so easily?"

"But what shall I do, Nirmal?" Charu struck her right hand on her forehead, cursing her destiny. "I have no choice. Marriage to the emperor and then death, is my fate. I cannot change that."

"Yes, you can," Nirmal reached for the note that had been cleverly concealed into the folds of her voluminous *ghagra*. "Read this. Jodhpuri Begum has sent it from Shahjahanabad."

Eyes widening, Charumati reached for the parchment paper. The message was brief and to the point, as though written by someone who understood the urgency of the situation.

"She has asked me to appeal to Rana Raj Singh for help." The Rajkumari looked up.

"She is wise," Nirmal took Charumati's hands in her own and pressed them gently. "You love the Rana, do you not, Charu?"

For the first time since the day her brother had broken the news about the proposal to her, Charumati smiled. After the dismal mood of the past few days, it was as if the sun had suddenly broken through a gloomy grey sky, instantly flooding the horizon with golden beams of light.

Nirmal smiled back at her friend. "You do not have to answer the question, Charu. But we must not waste time now. According to Jodhpuri Begum, it was the emperor's oldest daughter Zeb-un-Nissa, who informed him. Jodhpuri has also said that Zeb often intervenes on behalf of those who invite the emperor's wrath, but not in this case. Even his closest ministers have not tried to mediate. There is a unanimous feeling that you have committed a grave offence, and you need to be punished. Charu, you must write to the Rana immediately."

"Bhai sa will never forgive me for appealing to what he considers an enemy state." The Princess looked at her friend helplessly. "You know our relations with Mewar have been very tense since last year."

"This is a matter of your life, Charu. And he is the only one who can help you."

"But what if he does not come to my help? What if...."

"Not only is he really the only one who can, but it is also his duty as a *Rajputra* to fight righteously[46] and protect your honour," said Nirmal firmly. "How can he not? Consider the lineage he comes from Charu! Every one of his ancestors has steadfastly resisted the enemy.

Why, think of Rana Sanga with his one eye, one arm, one leg and eighty wounds all over his powerful body! Nothing deterred him from picking up the sword. It is not called 'Glorious Mewar' for nothing.[47] And Rana Raj Singh has never feared the emperor or the Mughal army. Quite the contrary I would think."

"You are right, Nirmal. The Rana is not afraid of anyone," Charumati agreed with her friend. "Do you remember? He had only just succeeded his father and taken over the *gaddi* when he announced that Chittor fort would be undergoing repairs. There was so much more to that announcement. It was an affirmation of the revival of Mewar's supremacy."

"Now that we agree that the Rana is both competent and duty bound, let us also concur that there is one more motivation for his intervention in this matter." Nirmal took a deep breath and then continued. "I am not a romantic like you, Charu, but I do happen to believe in love. And love is undoubtedly the biggest force."

"Perhaps I have been deluding myself all this time. How can I even be sure that he loves me like I love him?" Charu shook her head disconsolately, and Nirmal looked at her in surprise.

"You are the Princess of Kishengarh. Tales of your charm, beauty and goodness are known far and wide. It is highly improbable that he would not reciprocate your feelings. I am sure the Rana feels the same way about you as you do about him."

"Well, there is only one way to find out." Charumati re-read Jodhpuri Begum's letter and then quickly headed to her writing desk. "I will have to appeal to the Rana immediately."

"Just like Rukmani had appealed to Krishna. Then he arrived in his chariot and swept her away," Nirmal handed the quill to the Princess. "Write to him, Charu. Your brother will be getting ready to send his acceptance to the emperor. It is imperative that our message gets to the Rana before that letter reaches Shahjahanabad."

It was ironic that Nirmal should have said that because, at that very moment, Man Singh was writing his letter of acceptance to Aurangzeb. He had thought until he could think no more, deliberated with his most senior ministers for hours, and as a last resort imagined what the scenario would be like if he refused the emperor's proposal. That had actually helped him make up his mind. The scene of bloodshed and carnage that had unfolded in front of his closed eyes had been enough to send him rushing to his desk. Now, as he started writing the letter, Man Singh was aware that his hands were shaking considerably. So much so that the ink from the feathered quill had already blotched the thin parchment paper twice. Cursing under his breath, he tore up the paper and threw it into the bin. If he had to accept this dratted proposal, he at least wanted to do it with some shred of dignity. He took a deep breath. Then he picked up a clean cloth and wiped the nib of the quill with it. He took a couple of extra minutes to trim the top of the quill with a knife as well, so that the feather was just about nine inches in length. By then, his hands had steadied and with a deep breath, he pulled out a fresh parchment paper. He had already carefully reflected over his choice of words, so writing the letter didn't take long. He thanked the emperor for the honour and accepted the proposal on behalf of his sister Charumati. Then, before the nerves could hit him again, he folded the letter, slipped it into an envelope and sealed it. Calling one of his trusted darbaans, he handed the envelope to him, instructing that the letter be delivered to Emperor Aurangzeb without delay. "Send one of our fastest horsemen," he ordered.

"Ji Hukum," the darbaan bowed and, clutching the letter in his right hand, turned and marched down the hallway. As he watched him go, Raja Man Singh was acutely aware of a sense of finality that was slowly sinking in. There was no turning back now. The jewelled pagadi that he had removed earlier was lying on the diwan and he picked it up and placed it on top of his head. It was time to make the *ghoshana* in the durbar. "On an auspicious date next month, with the blessings of the Kuldevi, Rajkumari Charumati will marry the sixth Mughal Emperor, Aurangzeb of Shahjahanabad."

Even as Man Singh murmured the announcement over and over again, he realized that no amount of practice could completely conceal the regret in his voice, nor the tremor that had now returned to his hands.

CHAPTER 8

Even as Man Singh's messenger was getting ready to leave from Kishengarh toward Shahjahanabad, a horseman had already departed for Udaipur. The distance of more than three hundred kilometres could be comfortably covered by an able horseman in six days, but this man understood that he didn't have the luxury of time. Charumati had chosen well. Years ago, while learning how to ride as a child, she could have fallen off a particularly belligerent horse had it not been for this man. Deeply grateful for saving her, Charumati had been tying the sacred Rakhi on his wrist every year on Raksha Bandhan. The letter that he now carried might have been tightly sealed, but the man was aware of every word written in it, as well as the criticality of the message. For him, this was not merely an important message that had to be safely delivered to Udaipur. The letter concerned the honour of the Princess who he regarded as a sister. Not surprisingly, for him, it was therefore a matter of life and death.

Upon exiting Kishengarh fort, the horseman had barely ridden a few kilometres when he found himself in a dilemma. While the *pucca* road that led to Udaipur passed through Bijainagar, Bhilwara and Nathdwara, it was a safe and dependable route. On the other hand, the cut-off through the forested area was much shorter and, admittedly, much more dangerous. Everyone knew that the forests were the homes of dacoits and rebels, notorious for looting and killing.

As he stood there deliberating, he noticed a painter sitting in a shaded spot. He was laden with supplies of scrolls, brushes and colours. The horseman was no connoisseur of art but even he could see how skilled the man was, simply by observing the competence with which he was cleaning his brushes and mixing the colours. Even as he admired the resplendent reds, greens and yellows, the horseman was unaware that the colours were a result of days and days of arduous labour. The pigments were derived from natural sources and then endless hours of grinding, mixing and blending finally resulted in these perfect hues. The artist unfolded one of the scrolls. The partly finished painting was of a Holi celebration with Kishengarh fort as a backdrop. The spiritual Rajput style of painting that he specialized in was, of course, distinct from the more aristocratic artwork of the Mughal courts. Though now, political influence had ensured that a strong Mughal influence could be seen everywhere, including art.

The sound of a tinkling payal made the horseman turn around. A young woman in a light pink ghaghra choli was walking swiftly toward him. Her face was covered with a ghoonghat. For a moment, he thought it was the princess's best friend Nirmal since she was the one who usually wore pastel colours, but when she came closer and lifted the ghoonghat by a few inches, he realized that it was the Rajkumari herself. She had obviously exchanged clothes with her friend, so no one would recognize her.

"Rajkumari sa! What are you doing here?" He wondered how she had managed to walk all the distance from the entrance of the fort in the scorching sun. But then, most people in Kishengarh knew that underneath that delicate exterior, the Princess was much like any Rajput. Brave, valiant, fearless.

Indicating to the horseman to wait, the Princess looked around quickly. Once she was sure that nobody was watching, she ran to the painter. Nodding discreetly, Charumati held out her hand. The horseman watched in surprise as the painter pulled out a painting from his stack and handed it to her. Charumati gave him a gold coin and then approached the horseman. He glanced at the painting in her hand. It was of Lord Krishna and his wife Rukmini. The scene was a depiction of when Krishna had rescued Rukmini from Vidharbha so she wouldn't have to be forced into marrying Shishupal. In the painting, the couple was sitting side by side in the chariot. The arched eyebrows, lotus shaped eyes and sharply drawn features drew immediate attention to the faces, which had been done in a side profile. Rukmini had her arms around Krishna and in the background, her brother Rukmi and his army were chasing them. The wind-swept manes of the horses, the glimmer of Krishna's golden chariot and the adoring expression in Rukmini's eyes, had all been intricately detailed with the use of fine brush strokes and brilliant colours.

"When you give him the letter, please also give him this," Charumati rolled the painting into a scroll. "And tell him that if he does not come, I will have no choice but to end my life."

"Rajkumari sa, please do not...."

Charumati shook her head, a sudden, desperate look in her beautiful eyes. "Please hurry! There is not a single instant to waste. The emperor's *baraat* would be ready and waiting. No sooner will Bhai sa's messenger reach Shahjahanabad, than they will set off for Kishengarh. The Rana, on the other hand, is completely unaware of our circumstances. We might already be too late."

The horseman took the painting and tucked it safely into the leather pannier attached to the saddle. Then, without another word, he turned his horse and galloped swiftly toward the forest.

***

The fight had been organized on the muggy banks of the Jumna River in Delhi. The *akhada* was located here and was regularly used for animal fights as well as human wrestling. Mughal emperors over the decades were famed for having some of the most renowned wrestlers in their service. Iranians, Turks, Indians, the wrestlers received monthly salaries as well as rewards and decorations in the form of coveted robes of honour, gifts, even *jaghirs* and titles. During Jehangir's reign, a wrestler named Sher Ali from Bijapur had arrived at the royal court. One by one, he defeated all the wrestlers and impressed by his skill and strength, the emperor had bestowed him with the title of 'The wrestler of Dar al-Saltanat'.

Of course, the sport was not limited to those in service. Wrestling was considered to be a very manly sport and noblemen often participated as well. The wrestlers were coached by the ustaads and sometimes fights were organized between the noblemen and commoners.

Today, the akhada was being engaged for an elephant fight. The view of the grounds was the best from the secured pavilion where Emperor Aurangzeb was seated, along with the other members of the royal family. Noblemen and ministers, in order of rank were around the pavilion. Throngs of commoners, some nearly spilling out in anticipation, populated the area behind the thick ropes that had been used to cordon it off. After all, elephant fights were one of the most popular forms of entertainment, with the emperor holding the exclusive right to organize them. He usually also had his favourites, those were the ones who were privileged enough to have personal servants for their grooming and care. In fact, Aurangzeb's grandfather Jehangir had actually been known to own more than eleven thousand of these enormous beasts.[48] Elephants that were used for fights were trained by special *mahouts* or elephant trainers and were plied with copious amounts of *arak* and *mahua* before the fight. Their mahouts were equipped to keep them in control even as they hurled themselves at each other, frenzied with rage and inebriation. Despite the thorough training imparted to the mahouts, it was a dangerous sport. For the elephants, the mahouts and often even the spectators.

The fight started as always, with plenty of fanfare and excitement. The emperor though, seemed distracted. This was nothing new. Elephant fights did that to him. They brought back too many memories. Memories of a summer afternoon in Agra. He did, in fact, recall the exact month and year. June 1633,[49] by the banks of the same river. The crazed intoxicated beast charging at a young prince. The prince, terrorized out of his life by the sight of the elephant's mammoth trunk. He had never indulged in this kind of crazy entertainment. Why, oh why had he made an exception today? Those were the thoughts that had likely run through his mind as he kicked the sides of his horse, turned back and rushed to safety. Then his fifteen-year-old younger brother, so sure of himself, so hell bent on proving his brother's cowardice, that he unhesitatingly plunged into the fight. He would have done anything to show his older brother down that day. To prove his own mettle and his worth. The subsequent battle between him and the elephant. His horse losing his ground. The raised leg of the enraged beast, as he hurled it down, intent on crushing the life out of his opponent. And then with one sudden swift movement, the fifteen-year-old prince mustered up enough courage, grabbed his spear and with all his might, pierced it into the animal's eye. And then, the river of blood as the beast screamed and roared and finally, sank down into the ground, defeated. The blood was still flowing copiously out of his eye, as the spectators shrieked hysterically and then rushed to the ground to lift the young prince on their shoulders. They carried him all the way back to the pavilion, where his father sat, waiting, watching. Even while he smiled at his younger son and bestowed him with the honoured title of 'Bahadur', the fifteen-year-old Aurangzeb turned to look at his older brother Dara. And that had been the moment of truth for both of them. The bare, naked hatred they felt for each other could now no longer be denied.

A sneering look appeared on the emperor's face. To think that *buzdil* could ever have imagined that he was worthy of the Takht Murassa, the throne that was the seat of this mighty empire! The thought itself was ludicrous. He should have stuck with his music and art and books. He should have stayed within the confines of the court, never should have entered the battlefield. Then at least he wouldn't have met the end he did.

A sudden excited squeal of laughter snapped the emperor out of his reverie. The sound had come from one of the windows of the zenana. The emperor looked up. Dressed in a dark blue velvet robe, his eyes shining with anticipation, two-year-old Baby Mirza Mohammad Akbar was looking down at the ground where the elephants were fighting. His nanny was standing behind him, a doting look on her face. Aurangzeb's usually stern face tilted into a hint of a smile as he watched his fourth and most beloved son. His mother Dilras Banu had died right after giving birth to him, likely of puerperal fever due to complications from the delivery. That however, hadn't lessened his father's love for him.

"He is enjoying the fight, Aali Jaan," remarked Fazil Khan, the grand vizier. "He has obviously taken after his great-great-grandfather. Your highness, on the other hand, is much like the founder of our mighty empire, your great-great-great-grandfather. He was a military genius, a wonderful general. It is all documented very well in his memoirs, that he himself wrote."

"*The Baburnama*," Aurangzeb crossed his arms in front of his chest and nodded. "'*In the month of Ramadan of the year 899 [1494] and in the twelfth year of my age, I became ruler in the country of Farghana*,'" he quoted the first sentence as the minister smiled.

"It is a treasure trove. The first of its kind."

A roar of pain suddenly reverberated around the fort. Aurangzeb looked down from his vantage point in the pavilion. The defeated elephant lay on the ground, its enormous body covered with bloody wounds. Turning to the prime minister, Aurangzeb said, "The end is never pretty. The mightier always wins. As my great-great-great-grandfather used to say, 'The unconquerable will and courage, never to submit or yield.'"

"He was certainly to be admired," agreed Fazil Khan. "Speaking of which, he did not believe in waiting. He believed in acting."

Aurangzeb rose from his seat. "I understand we have still not received any response from Kishengarh."

"They are fools." The prime minister rolled his eyes.

"Yes, because now my patience is beginning to run thin. Private appearance tomorrow morning. I need all the mansabdars to be present. We have much planning to do."

"It will be child's play," the prime minister shrugged nonchalantly. He was just about to express how unconcerned he was about fighting a kingdom so small, so inconsequential, when the emperor put a hand up to stop him. Even as his eyes bore into the minister's face, the man quickly looked down. The sharp contrast of those dark eyes against his white alabaster skin usually made most people want to stop and stare but those who knew him closely, never ever dared to look into those eyes too long. It was almost as though the darkest phantoms of the most complex mind lurked there, in those eyes.

"Comfort and complacency are the evils that numb the mind." The emperor pointed to the fighting ground. "Qawii Khan was the stronger of the two elephants. Yet he was defeated today."

"*Gustakhi maaf, Aali Jaan.*" Fazil Khan bowed his head. "It is a unanimous opinion that the Mughal cavalry is invincible in the subcontinent. Kishengarh is a tiny kingdom with nothing to speak of."

"These are the Rajputs we are talking about. Bravery, fortitude, sacrifice... these are in their blood. We should know, should we not? After all, look at our own senior general, Mirza Raja Jai Singh. Thoroughly skilled in the arts of armour, with a fierce military temperament. Never forget the way he defeated Shuja and chased him back to Bengal. His military prowess and analytical expertise have been proved time and again.[50] And there are several like him. While he has sworn his loyalty to the imperial throne, there are others who might actually dare to stand up to us."

"I still believe, Aali Jaan, that Raja Man Singh cannot be that stupid. Do you really think he will refuse the proposal?"

"I am not talking about Man Singh. In fact, I am very sure that we can expect to receive his letter of acceptance anytime now. However, I am also equally sure that Rajkumari Charumati will do everything in her power to fight back. If her brother does not support her, she will seek other sources of assistance."

Mounting his horse to ride the short distance back to the palace, he indicated to the prime minister to ride alongside. Fazil Khan who knew the emperor well, understood that he wasn't in a mood to make any more conversation and they rode in silence until they reached the palace gates. The emperor's personal *ghulam* was waiting there. He had appeared as soon as the sounds of the horses' hooves could be heard in the distance.

"Call all the mansabdars to the private audience hall tomorrow morning before the *zuhr*." The emperor nodded to the minister and then turned to the ghulam. "Send a message to Nawab Bai that I will be joining her for dinner tonight."

"As you wish, Aali Jaan."

Even as he watched the emperor ride into the palace, the prime minister couldn't help thinking that the emperor visiting one of his wives for dinner was not a common occurrence. Nawab Bai was his second wife but despite giving him his oldest son, she had played second fiddle to Dilras Banu until the time the latter was alive. Even after her death, the emperor much preferred to spend his time in religious and administrative pursuits rather than with his other wives.[51] But then it was common knowledge that the emperor did not possess the amorous demeanour that had been almost second nature to his grandfather and even his father. Aurangzeb had been fond of his chief wife and had held her in high regard, but he just wasn't given to sentimentalism. Except that one time. The prime minister smiled inwardly. He'd heard the rumour of course. Zainabadi Mahal, named after the place where he first glimpsed her. She'd been a slave girl of Mir Khalil, the son-in-law of Shah Jahan's grand vizier. Mir Khalil had been sent to the Deccan as chief of the artillery. The year was 1652, and it was during his own vice royalty to the Deccan, that Prince Aurangzeb saw her for the first time in a garden. She was plucking a mango from a tree and rumour had it that the prince instantly fell in love. So much so that the love affair actually lasted several months. Captivated by her musical talent as well as her beauty, the otherwise austere prince even agreed to taste wine for the first time, at her insistence. It was supposed to be a test of love and she stopped him at the last moment, but his willingness to go to any length to please her, proved how intensely infatuated he was.[52] Her death two years later had a profound impact on him, to the extent that his health also got affected.[53] It was perhaps the one and only time that he might have actually experienced love or anything remotely close to it. Perhaps it was no wonder then, that he hadn't married as many times as several of his ancestors.

"All things considered, there is certainly room for one more begum in the shahi harem," murmured the prime minister to himself then. "I must ask Princess Zeb to start making arrangements for Charumati's arrival. It will not be long now."

Chapter 9

The emperor's palace was divided into three sections; the prayer room, bedrooms and dressing rooms. The symbol of justice was imprinted here as well. Every morning, the emperor would awaken and then the first thing that he did was to get his dreams recorded on paper. Sometimes those dreams were so fascinating that renowned court artists could create paintings based on them. Jehangir for instance, once had a dream of Shah Abbas Safavid of Iran. This was during a time when relations between the two empires were strained over the Qandahar Fortress and in his dream, the Mughal emperor saw himself and the Shah embracing each other. He subsequently commissioned the famed court painter, Abu'l Hasan to create a painting based on the dream. Expectedly, even though the painting was brilliantly done, it was a highly biased and partial representation with the Shah being shown almost as though he were deferring to his Mughal counterpart.[54] In any case, the dreams of the emperor were regarded as a manifestation of his subconscious thoughts and aspirations, and were unfailingly recorded with as much detail and accuracy as possible.

After completing his morning prayers, the emperor would commence his daily activities. The day would begin with *jharokha darshan,*[55] the practice of greeting the public from a predetermined jharokha or window. This system had been started by Akbar[56] to let his people know that he was alive and well. Sometimes he would even let down a thread and people would tie their grievances to it, particularly those that required the emperor's urgent attention. His son Jehangir took the practice a step further by installing a chain of justice, linking his jharokha balcony to a post by the Jumna so that anyone seeking justice could ring the bells attached to the chain. Shah Jahan had continued the practice as well and the only time he missed appearing at the jharokha was when he had been taken ill. Rumours immediately began circulating that the emperor was dead, and it was only when he finally appeared at the window, that the people were reassured. His son Aurangzeb however, had not approved of this practice from the very beginning. He considered it un-Islamic, a form of idol worship. He often thought of discontinuing it, but it had only been a couple of years since his coronation, so for now he carried on, albeit relatively disinterestedly.

Everything else notwithstanding, two of the most significant tasks that the emperor had to carry out everyday were the public audience in the Diwan-i-Aam and the private audience in the Diwan-i-Khas. It was what kept him connected to his people as well as his ministers and facilitated him to be an able administrator and exerciser of justice. Every Mughal emperor also kept aside a day of the week for personally attending to judicial cases. Akbar had reserved Thursday, Jehangir Tuesday and Shah Jahan had reserved Wednesday. Aurangzeb had continued with Wednesday as the official day of justice. On this day, no public audience was held.

However, on that particular day, despite the fact that it was not a Wednesday, Aurangzeb had unceremoniously called off the public audience. It was the upcoming private audience in the Diwan-i-Khas with his most senior ministers, noblemen and mansabdars, that he wanted to solely concentrate on.

The Hall of Private Audience, or the Diwan-i-Khas as it was called, was a spectacular vision, any time of the day. A ninety feet by sixty-seven feet rectangular marble structure with a gold inlaid ceiling and interceding arches that rose majestically from gilded piers designed with floral motifs, it was so grand that even those who saw it on a regular basis couldn't stop themselves from marvelling at its sight.[57] The Takht Murassa was in the centre of the hall. Over a thousand kilos of gold had gone into constructing it and it was covered in precious stones all over, making it twice as valuable as Shah Jahan's masterpiece creation, the Taj Mahal. Several diamonds of historical significance were studded into it, including the 186-karat Kohinoor or 'mountain of light'. The fact that Jehangir's throne had simply been a rectangular block of black basalt made the new takht seem even more extravagant. Ironically, it was the least extravagant Mughal emperor who now occupied it.

If the opulence of the Diwan-i-Khas was special, then its purpose was also equally exclusive. Matters of the state, reception of foreign dignitaries, fresh appointments both at the centre and in different parts of the empire, issue and dispatch of *farmans* and *khilats*, review of ranks, discussion about the empire's financial affairs, critical military dialogue, this is where it all happened. Sometimes animal parades with exotic animals like tamed tigers, painted elephants, Uzbek dogs, *neel-gais*, as well as *gurz-bardar* or entertainment by mace bearers were also on the agenda.[58] Additionally, it was court etiquette to offer presents in the form of *peshkash, nisar* and *nazar*, to the emperor. These were presented by the *wakils* of the noblemen.[59] As far as entry was concerned, it was restricted to the highest-ranking ministers, courtiers and ambassadors. They also had to unfailingly follow a rule.

It was a simple one, actually. It was mandatory for anyone seeking admission into this private durbar to wear *ittar*, the perfume that had become so popular since the time Noor Jehan's mother, Asmat Begum, first learnt how to make it from flowers.

Now, as the invitees started congregating inside the hall on that particular morning, a heavenly aroma of sandalwood, *oud*, musk, and rose wafted through the air. Hushed voices could be heard as the ministers and noblemen quietly conferred amongst themselves, speculating about the subject of today's audience. Everyone understood that when an urgent audience was called, it had to be a matter of political or military criticality. Barely a few minutes had passed when the durbaan at the entrance announced the arrival of the emperor.

Even as sounds of 'Long live Alamgir' and 'Hail to Alamgir' resonated around the hall, trumpets and cymbals heralded his entry. Dressed in a simply embroidered white kurta, churidar and an embellished brocade robe and turban, Aurangzeb walked down the carpeted hall and took his place on the throne. His only jewellery that morning was a pearl and emerald necklace, and in his right hand, he held his *misbaha* of a hundred prayer beads. Thirty-three for *Tasbeeh*, thirty-three for *Tahmeed* and thirty-four for *Takbeer*.

As per court protocol, the *omara* and ambassadors had congregated just below the throne. The enclosure where they were standing was demarcated with silver railings. Mansabdars and others stood at a slight distance.

With a nod, the emperor indicated to Raja Jai Singh to step forward. The general immediately complied. Head bowed, he offered the traditional Islamic greeting.

"*Mughliya Saltnat ka iqbaal buland rahe.*"

"Mirza Raja," the emperor leaned back into the throne. "In what year did your military career with us begin?"

The general knew that the emperor was well aware of the answer, as he was of most things. Trying not to worry about the motive behind this seemingly innocuous question, he answered. "Aali Jaan, my military career started in 1627, with the accession of your father as emperor."

"And I must say that over the years you played a pivotal role in his court.[60] Then, impressed with your response to the Afghan rebels, he made you a commander of 4000. You once again proved your mettle during the Deccan campaign in 1636. And yet again in the one against the Gond kingdoms. You were made a commander and declared a rising star. Of course, your true moment of triumph came with the surrender of the Fort of Kandahar to us. My father bestowed you with the title of Mirza Raja."

There was pin drop silence in the durbar. It was obvious that the emperor had not asked them to gather here solely to discuss Mirza Raja's career. They all waited for him to continue.

"You were appreciated by everyone except one. He, who was hostile to you from the very beginning. He, who blamed you entirely for the failure to recover Kandahar in 1649 and 1652. Later, he even deprived you of your rightful promotions and rewards. Yet, in the war of 1657, he chose to make you Commander of 6000 and send you East. I have always wondered why he did that, Mirza Raja. Why?"

For a moment, Jai Singh wondered whether the emperor wished him to respond. Then, shaking his head slightly as though in mock disbelief, Aurangzeb answered his own question. "Considering how incompetent he otherwise was, it is astounding how he managed to recognize your military astuteness. That, perhaps, was the only smart thing Dara did during that war. Even though it was too little, too late. You of course, were much too perceptive to support a loser, Mirza Raja. You knew he did not have the makings of a badshaah. You wanted the reins of this great empire to be in the most capable hands. You chose wisely. But then, you *are* wise and that is why I have faith in you."

"Shukriya, Aali Jaan. It is my honour to serve you."

"Why do we fight battles, Mirza Raja?"

Jai Singh blinked, taken aback. "Battles, Aali Jaan?"

"Yes. What are the motivations, the provocations?"

"Power, Aali Jaan," offered the general then, even as he tried to wrack his brains to come up with the best possible answer.

"Only power?"

"Power, honour, prestige, glory."

For an emperor who was known to hardly ever smile, the slight upward tilt of his lips was enough to convey that he was indeed happy with the general's answer.

"And what should we do if someone tries to mar that glory, that honour?"

"We need to teach them a lesson," Jai Singh's voice was solid, resolute. "One that will set an example so nobody ever dares to do so again."

"Good. I am glad to know that as usual, we are in agreement Mirza Raja. Like I said, you are a wise, perceptive man. Now while I am aware that we are in an enviable position as far as size and strength are concerned, I do know that like me, you do not believe in being complacent. Call a meeting of all the mansabdars," he paused to look at some of them, and several heads nodded in agreement at once.

"Ask them to put the troops together," he continued then to Jai Singh. "They must also take stock of the Dakhili troops. You will personally oversee the situation with the Ahadis. I am sure I do not need to tell you that the cavalry needs to be given special attention."

"Yes, Aali Jaan," Jai Singh did not ask for further details. The instructions were clear enough. The emperor however, had not missed the quizzical expression on his general's face. His eyes quickly scanned the faces of the ministers assembled in the front of the hall.

"*Diwan-i-Ala?*"

Here in court, he always addressed him by his title.

Fazil Khan stepped forward.

"What was that quote used by the English diplomat who visited a few months ago? Something about a mountain, was it not?"

"To make a mountain out of a molehill," the Prime Minister smiled. "It was first used by a famous Greek satirist."

"Thank you for refreshing my memory," the emperor turned back to Jai Singh.

"What concerns me might well be a molehill. Though you know me well. I believe in the reverse. Never make a molehill out of a mountain."

"I understand, Aali Jaan. It will be done," Bowing, Jai Singh stepped back.

The emperor then nodded to Raja Raghunath Singh to come forward. As *Diwan-i-Wazarat*, it was his responsibility to oversee the revenue, taxes, and the imperial treasury. Along with Jai Singh, Raja Raghunath Singh was also one of the Hindu ministers who occupied an influential position in Alamgir's court.[61] He had been a powerful minister in Shah Jahan's court and Alamgir who had a genuine regard for him, had decided to keep him on.[62]

"Raja Raghunath, I know there is no scope for any error in your calculations and judgement. I need a precise understanding of the current state of the shahi khazana. And I need this at once."

"Very well, Aali Jaan."

Just then a messenger, escorted by two soldiers, was brought to the doorway of the hall. He hadn't yet stepped inside, but as he looked around with wide eyes, it was palpable how awe-struck he was even by the magnificence of the entrance. It was evident from his clothes and manner that he had come from one of the Rajput states.

"Aali Jaan, a messenger has arrived from Kishengarh," announced the accompanying soldier. "He brings an urgent message from Raja Man Singh."

The emperor nodded to Fazil Khan, who in turn signalled to the messenger to enter the hall.

As the messenger started walking toward the end of the hall where the emperor was seated on the throne, there were hushed whispers from the ministers who thronged both sides of the passageway. The emperor however, remained as poker faced as ever, his expression giving nothing away. The quick conspiratorial look that he exchanged with Fazil Khan went unnoticed as all eyes were fixed on the messenger and the scroll in his hand. He finally stopped a few feet away from the pedestal on which the throne was placed. The pedestal was also often described as the *qibla* to indicate the direction faced by Muslims during prayer.

Bowing reverentially, the messenger greeted the emperor and conveyed the Raja's deep respects. He then sought the emperor's permission to read out the *paigam*.

"*Paigam pesh kiya jaye*," instructed Fazil Khan at the emperor's approval.

The messenger opened the scroll and started reading.

"It was an honour and a privilege for us to receive Emperor Alamgir's proposal of marriage for my sister, Rajkumari Charumati. With the greatest joy in my heart, I accept this marriage proposal sent by Emperor Alamgir for Rajkumari Charumati. We hope that by way of this *Haldi Chandan*, Kishengarh and Shahjahanabad will remain forever engaged in a relationship of trust, solidarity and friendship."

Then as per tradition, the messenger proffered a betel leaf with gold coins and flowers to the emperor. Fazil Khan stepped forward and accepted the offering on the emperor's behalf. With a bow, the messenger thanked him, and Fazil Khan promised that they would soon arrive in Kishengarh to escort the Princess back to Shahjahanabad where the wedding would take place. The *saqnac* in the form of an elaborate necklace encrusted with polkis, rubies and emeralds, was given to the messenger and with that, the marriage was confirmed. Rajkumari Charumati of Kishengarh was now officially betrothed to Emperor Alamgir.

Even as the sounds of '*Mubarak ho, mubarak ho,*' reverberated around the Diwan-i-Khas, Fazil Khan glanced up at the emperor seated on the takht. It was the smallest sign, so imperceptible that only his closest ones would have understood. And Fazil Khan understood. Do not make a molehill out of a mountain. Do not trust. Do not let your guard down. Yes, despite this recent development, the earlier plans would remain unchanged. Now, of course, they were merely a precaution. *Inshallah,* there would be no need to action them. The proposal had been accepted. The baraat would go to Kishengarh and return with Charumati's *doli*. And never again would anyone, anywhere, dare to wish ill for the mighty Alamgir or for this great empire.

Chapter 10

When Charumati's trusted messenger took a decision to take the shortcut through the forest instead of the safe route via Bhilwara, he was aware of the apparent dangers of his decision. Everyone knew that the forests were teeming with ferocious river crocodiles, savage hyenas and wild jackals but that wasn't the only hazard. Paucity of money and societal rejection had turned several of the locals into rebels and dacoits, who now inhabited the forests. The density of the woodlands and the lack of law enforcement made these forests a perfect hideout for them. Notorious for kidnapping, looting and sometimes even killing those who dared to set foot onto their turf, the dacoits were particularly belligerent toward anyone coming from the royal palace.

And then, there was the legend of the *chudail*. He'd heard it hundreds of times, everyone had. Some believed that she'd died during childbirth whereas others claimed that she'd been tortured and driven to suicide by her in-laws. Whatever the cause, almost everyone agreed that she now wandered in the forest, looking for revenge. Her targets were usually men and even though she was hideous to look at, she could transform herself into a beautiful woman to entice men. Then she would suck all their blood out and leave them to die. None of the bodies had been found but many a traveller had disappeared in these parts of the jungle. Of course, she usually appeared at night and if he was quick, he would be out of the area before sundown.

Muttering the *Hanuman Chalisa* under his breath, the horseman rode on. Day or night, this part of the forest felt ominous. Some of the trees were so tall that they seemed to close in completely, blocking out all sunlight and making it impossible to see the path ahead. Shadows appeared, then disappeared, and the howling of wolves broke the eerie silence now and then.

A gun shot suddenly rang out, sending a flock of myenas fluttering down from the trees. The horseman was used to hearing gun shots around the palace in Kishengarh but here in this silent forest, it sounded three times as loud, and he almost fell off his horse. Clutching the reins, he looked around in terror.

Half a dozen men on horses appeared from seemingly nowhere, surrounding him on all sides. Their unkempt moustaches, black turbans and the guns they brandished, were all evident of the fact that they were dacoits. Their faces were covered with black cloth, and it was hard to tell one from the other.

One of the men pointed his gun at the horseman, instructing him to step down.

"Where do you come from and where are you going?"

The horseman understood that he was most likely the chief of the gang. He was also well aware that he had to tell the truth. They would undoubtedly search him and as soon as they found the Rajkumari's letter, they would know his plans.

"I come from Kishengarh Fort. I am on my way to Udaipur."

"Search him!" the chief commanded two of the other men who immediately got down from their horses.

"Are you not aware that strangers are not welcome in these parts of the forest?" The chief looked at him suspiciously even as the rough hands of the other men frisked him from top to bottom. "And if we have reason to believe that you might be a threat, you will not get out of here alive. Be very sure of that."

"*Bhavani ma ki kasam,* I am telling the truth."

"*Sardar,* this is all he is carrying," one of the men brought the horseman's belongings to the chief and handed them over to him. "One gold chain, a few silver coins, a painting and a letter."

The chief rummaged through the things. After pocketing the silver coins and gold chain, he opened the letter. His eyes widened in astonishment as he read it.

"So, the Rajkumari is appealing to the Rana of Udaipur for help. I had assumed that the gold chain was your most valuable asset, but I was wrong. This letter is worth its weight in gold."

"Please! Let me deliver the letter to the Rana. Pray allow me to fulfil my promise to the Rajkumari. It is my duty."

"Duty? Duty!" the chief of the dacoits threw his head back and laughed. "Do you recall the time when the local villagers had begged Raja Man Singh to do something about the way those rich landowners were treating their poor tenants? Was that not his responsibility? And you have the nerve to stand here and talk about duty?"

"This is for the Rajkumari," the horseman wrung his hands together and went down on his knees. "She is a gentle soul and has done no harm to anyone."

"No, I have made up my mind," the chief put the letter into the pocket of his *kurta*. "This will be sold to the badshaah of Shahjahanabad for a tidy sum. We will use the money to get the daughter of a poor blacksmith married. Their need is much greater than the whims and fancies of these royals. And as for you..." He raised his gun and pointed it directly at the horseman.

An arrow suddenly appeared, missing the chief's hand by

barely a millimetre. The startled chief dropped the gun and looked around frantically.

"Let the poor man go! Now!"

The voice was like nothing any of them had ever heard before. It was deep, powerful, commanding. A voice that was used to being obeyed immediately.

"Who are you?" demanded the chief. "Show yourself!"

There was a rustle from behind a copse of trees. A tall broad man, sitting atop a white horse came into view. The messenger stared at his determined, handsome face. He'd seen this face in numerous paintings before and though he'd never met him or even come face-to-face with him, he recognized him instantly. It was Rana Raj Singh of Mewar. But what was he doing in these parts?

"I don't like to repeat myself." Despite the considerable distance between them, the Rana's voice rang out clearly. Removing another arrow from the quiver on his back, he took aim. "No more warnings. And be advised, I never miss a target."

The chief and his men looked enraged. Only one of them seemed uneasy. Like the messenger, he too had recognized the Rana.

"You dare to come into our domain and threaten us! I will teach you a lesson. Kill him now!" the chief commanded one of his men.

The man took aim but before he could even touch the trigger of his gun, an arrow pierced through his forehead, killing him immediately. Even as the dead man fell from his horse and slumped to the ground, the chief stared at him in astounded silence. With a roar of fury, he grabbed his own gun and tried to aim it at the Rana.

Another arrow whistled past the other men, this time slicing through the chief's heart. Clutching the arrow with his hands, he collapsed on his horse. A pool of sticky blood slowly started to gather around him, drenching the mane of the horse.

There was total silence as the other dacoits stared at the Rana in astonishment. With their chief dead, they were now at a complete loss about what to do next. Besides, the Rana was already poised to strike again, his bow and arrow ready to take aim at anyone who would dare to move so much as an inch.

"Save yourselves while you have the opportunity."

He was as still as a statue, his eyes faultlessly trained to react to any movement. "If you leave now, you will leave unharmed."

Three of the remaining four men turned their horses and fled into the forest. The sound of the horses' hooves could be heard for a few seconds as they galloped away. Then there was pin drop silence. The Rana stared at the lone dacoit who had chosen to stay.

"It seems you do not value your life. I do not know you, and have no reason to wish you harm. However, if you try any tricks, I will not spare you. And believe me when I say this. I never miss my target."

"I know that, Rana ji. I am well versed with your archery skills. As I am with your horse riding and sword fighting abilities."

The Rana raised his eyebrows. "You know me?"

"I know you very well, Rana ji. I am from Udaipur and your family is the reason that I can proudly claim to belong to Mewar. Most of the Rajput states have acceded to the Mughals. Mewar is one of the few still standing strong. You have truly done justice to your family's honour, Rana ji."

"What is your name?"

"Manik Lal. And I have nothing but respect for you in my heart."

"What are you doing here in this forest then? You are a dacoit, are you not?"

"Suffice it to say that when a human being falls on hard times and his basic survival is challenged, he might not have too many choices. This is not the life I used to lead," he paused and looked at the Rana who was still watching at him suspiciously. After all, most dacoits were outlaws who rebelled against the rulers and the kingdom. How could he trust this man merely on the basis of his words?

"Allow me to prove my loyalty to you, Rana ji. I am a Rajput and I mean what I say." Without a moment's hesitation, Manik Lal pulled out a knife from his pocket and cut off the index finger of his left hand.

The Rana lowered his bow and arrow. The man could have easily escaped, he'd given him the opportunity. He had instead, chosen to do this. Blood was flowing copiously from his hand, but he seemed completely undeterred.

The Rana turned to the messenger and nodded, "Retrieve your belongings."

"Ji Hukum!"

The chain and silver coins were strewn on the ground where they had fallen when the chief had died. The messenger gathered them up and slipped them back into his pannier. Then he fished out the painting and Charumati's letter from the dead chief's pocket. Turning to the Rana, he sought his permission. "May I approach you, Hukum?"

"Yes," the Rana nodded.

With rapid strides, the messenger crossed the distance to where the Rana was waiting. "Despite my earlier ordeal, I am glad that I took this route instead of the safe one. You might find this astonishing, but I was actually traveling to Udaipur to see you Hukum."

"To see me?" the Rana stared at him. "Is everything all right? You are coming from Kishengarh, are you not?"

"Ji Hukum. I have a message for you from the palace."

"Well, I did not think there would be much that Man Singh would wish to speak with me about," the Rana shrugged. "Since he obviously made it clear that relations between Kishengarh and Udaipur are not on the best terms. Besides, his allegiance with Shahjahanabad does not impress me at all. Yet you say that you have a message from him. That confounds me, to be perfectly honest."

"The message is not from Raja Man Singh," the messenger proffered the letter to the Rana. "Please read this, Hukum. You will understand what I am talking about."

The Rana took the letter and opened it. As he started reading, a troubled look appeared on his face. This was promptly replaced with an expression of distress as the full enormity of the situation was revealed. The Princess had explained the circumstances in no uncertain terms. Yes, she had insulted and offended Emperor Aurangzeb by crushing his painting under the sole of her jooti. He had sent a marriage proposal for her which her brother had had no choice but to accept. And yes, she expected the Rana to save her honour by taking her back to Udaipur with him and marrying her. She had professed her ardent love for him in the letter, which the Rana knew, couldn't have been easy. She'd ended the letter with a promise that if he didn't come to her rescue, she would have no choice but to end her life.

"This is terrible, simply terrible!" he exclaimed. His eyes quickly ran over the elegant handwriting again to make sure that he hadn't missed anything.

Folding his hands, the messenger said, "Yes, it is a very grave situation, Hukum. Will you help her?"

"I consider your question to be an insult. I am a Rajput. Do you really think I would ever turn down a plea like this? Mewar has never shied away from fighting for what is right. It was way back in the eighth century when we were attacked for the first time by Muhammad Bin Qasim of the Arab Caliphate. After conquering Sindh, he set his sights on Mewar but had to accept a crushing defeat. That was just the beginning. Fighting for pride and honour runs in our blood. It is my duty to protect the Rajkumari."

He did not mention that he would gladly lay down his life for the woman he loved.

"I apologize, Hukum. Please forgive me," the messenger bowed his head. "However, there is one more thing that I must tell you. Raja Man Singh has already sent his acceptance to Shahjahanabad."

"That means we have no time to waste!" The Rana put the letter into his pocket. "We Rajputs are courageous, not stupid. We cannot get the troops ready in such a short time. Aurangzeb's men would already be on their way to Kishengarh by now. And with the limited men we have handy, an open encounter is out of the question. We will have to ambush them on their way back. Perhaps lie in wait somewhere close to this forest."

"Then I would be glad to be of assistance, Rana ji," Manik Lal joined them. "I know every inch of this area like the back of my hand. You can trust me."

"I have no doubt in your ability to guide us through these parts. Nor in your loyalty." The Rana slapped Manik Lal on the back. "Mount your horse. Let us plan as we ride," He turned to the messenger. "You can return to Kishengarh now. Rest assured, we will let no harm come to the Princess."

"There is one last thing, Hukum. I must hand it over to you." The messenger held out the painting. "The Rajkumari asked me to give you this."

The Rana took the scroll and opened it. A smile spread across his face as he saw the painting depicting Princess Rukmini being driven away in a golden chariot by Lord Krishna. A patron of good art, the Rana could see that great attention had been paid to the minutest details by the painter.

"This is a beautiful work. It is evident that the Rajkumari is a connoisseur like me."

The Rana rolled the painting back into a scroll and returned it to the messenger.

The messenger looked confused. "What happened, Hukum? Did I offend you in some way or...."

"Not at all," the Rana patted the man's hand. "I have understood what the Rajkumari wishes to convey. She has likened herself to Rukmini and me to Lord Krishna. That is an enormous honour for me, the greatest perhaps. How can I accept this painting until I have carried out the duty that she has entrusted me with?"

"But, Hukum..."

"Please keep the painting with you. I will accept this only after I have taken Rajkumari Charumati safely back to Udaipur and made her my queen. But do not tell her this. I will tell her myself when I meet her."

With that, the Rana tightened the reins and gently prodded his horse with his leg. Turning the animal, he then rode back the way he had come, Manik Lal following him closely. The messenger watched for a few minutes and then, when the duo had finally disappeared from sight, he got on his horse to make his way back to Kishengarh.

Chapter 11

The uphill road leading to Kishengarh fort was a long one, but the entire stretch had been thoroughly cleaned and then strewn with flowers. Now the evening air was resplendent with the fragrance of fresh roses and marigolds. The main entrance had been adorned with *toran* garlands, and hundreds of *diyas* glowed and shimmered in the twilight. On the top of the entry gates stood two turbaned men in traditional Rajasthani poshak, playing *nagaras*. These enormous kettle drums that were played in the standing position were associated with auspicious occasions and festivals. Just beyond the entry gates, women with ghoonghats that completely covered their faces, held in their hands, intricate silver trays piled high with even more flowers.

There were hundreds of jaali jharokhas in the fort palace and positioned at one of them, Charumati and Nirmal stood watching as the Mughal contingent entered the fort and the Rajputs welcomed them with a generous shower of petals. Right in front, leading the contingent was a soldier, holding the official imperial *alam*, representative of the Mughal empire. The *Shir-u-Khurshid*. A deep moss green in colour, it displayed the image of a lion holding his head up with pride, along with a sunburst or *shamsha* in the background. Shamshas held a position of supreme significance in all Mughal insignia. Banners, flags, coins, shields, manuscripts and even Mughal thrones were often decorated with these sparkling golden sunbursts. The Mughals who had descended from the Mongol Khans, traced their lineage back to the sun and to them, the ruler of their empire was representative of the sun itself. Even Alamgir's father Shah Jahan, had later been addressed as 'The All-Powerful Sun' and Akbar had often been referred to as 'His Majesty the Sun'. According to the grand vizier and author of the *Akbarnama*, Abul Fazal, even Akbar's accession to the throne had concurred with an extremely auspicious moment and his reign would be protected by 'the Sultan of the Spheres' or the Sun itself.

This solar symbolism in fact, was in no way restricted to the emperor only. Important female members of the imperial family were given the same prestige. Jehangir's wife, Mehr-un-Nissa, later came to be known as Noor Jehan which literally meant 'The Light of the World'. The current emperor's mother Mumtaz Mahal too was often called 'The Sun of Modesty' and his older sister Jahanara 'The Light of the Imperial Chamber'.[63]

Now, behind the man proudly holding the imperial alam, walked more soldiers carrying other Mughal insignia. They were followed closely by the rest of the contingent. It had taken them only five days to cover the distance from Shahjahanabad, but the instruction had been to move fast. There were hundreds of them and at first it would have appeared to any spectator as though it was a never-ending army. The sheer numbers were certainly overwhelming, and the sight might have been frightening to anyone. Despite her earlier sense of distress, at that moment, Charumati simply felt incensed at the sight of them entering her palace.

"How dare they, Nirmal! How dare!" Her face was red with rage and her eyes almost as though they were on fire. "And look at Bhai sa!

Welcoming them with garlands! He should be ashamed of himself."

Raja Man Singh and all the senior ministers of his court were present at the entry gates. The obligatory smiles on their faces had momentarily managed to conceal the distress they had been feeling for days.

"*Swagat hai!*" With folded hands, the Raja stepped forward. "It is a matter of great honour for me to be able to welcome you to Kishengarh. May this union signify a strong bond of friendship, cooperation and mutual support between the Rajputs and the Mughals."

He then led them into the palace and the group of musicians who had been stationed at the entrance picked up their instruments. Man Singh had called the finest musicians in Kishengarh and within seconds, the melodious sounds of the *shehnai, manjira* and dhol resonated around the hills that surrounded the fort. Considered extremely auspicious, shehnai music was customary on important occasions like ceremonies in the temples of royal courts or marriages.

"I actually cannot help but find it rather strange," Nirmal looked at Charumati. "That the Shehnai always evokes a sense of melancholy in me."

"Well, the shehnai is regarded as a means to communicate with God. Perhaps that is the reason it is played at religious occasions, weddings and funerals alike," Charumati laughed bitterly. "Though that makes perfect sense. After all, today is my funeral, is it not?"

"Charu!" Nirmal grasped her friend's hand. "Do not despair! You know the Rana will never let you down."

"Where is he, then?" In a sudden desperate gesture, Charumati clutched her hands to her hair and shrieked. "They have already entered the palace, Nirmal! Hundreds of them, all with one sole objective in mind. To take me back to Shahjahanabad to that Badshah!" She spat the last word out, her voice trembling with fury.

"I just hope and pray that our messenger reached Udaipur in time. And that the Rana was there to receive your letter, Charu."

There was a soft knock on the door and both girls hurriedly stepped away from the window. Two daasis entered, bearing in their hands, enormous silver *thaalis*. They were Charumati's personal daasis, and had been waiting on her since she was a little girl. Laid out on the first thaali was a heavily embellished ghagra choli and odhni. The second one held the royal family's ancestral wedding jewellery including Charumati's grandmother's wedding choker, *bajuband*, toe rings, anklets, nose ring, *raani haar, kamarband* and *maang* tikka. Nestled on one side, were the traditional ivory and gold bangles or *hathi dant ka chooda* that were worn by every Rajput bride. The bangles were not simply ornaments. Ivory bangles held a significance as far as a woman's married life was concerned and were particularly crucial in ensuring childbirth as well.[64] Given to the bride by her maternal uncle, these were the bangles that allowed the bridal couple to perform the seven steps around the ceremonial fire. In her case, of course, there would be no seven steps nor a sacred fire. The thought brought instant tears to Charumati's eyes. Never had she imagined that her marriage would take place this way.

With bowed heads, the daasis placed the thaalis on the centre table. Then the older of the two folded her hands and spoke to Charumati. "Rajkumari sa, the Raja has sent this. You are to adorn this *joda* for the *vidai*."

"Has a time been ascertained for the haldi?"

It was Nirmal who had asked the question. Charumati was too overwhelmed at that moment to speak.

"Ji Hukum. The haldi has been scheduled for tomorrow morning. There is also a pooja that is to take place at the *Kuldevi's* temple."

It was the belief of the family that the Kuldevi or family deity was constantly watching over them, protecting their interests. As the foremost guardian of their fortune and honour, she had to be revered first, before any of the other ceremonies could be initiated.[65]

"As for the Mughals," continued the daasi. "Their food, entertainment and living arrangements for the night have been personally taken care of by the Raja. Chess, *chaupar, patang baazi,* music and dance. It is going to be a grand celebration all day and night."

"And do not forget the food," added the other daasi. "I have not seen such a feast being prepared for a very long time. *Dal bati churma, kir sangri, pithore, kachori, gatte ki sabzi, rabri ghewar, jalebi, malpua...*"

"There is nothing surprising about that," interrupted the older woman with a smile. "Obviously the Raja will leave no stone unturned as far as the wedding is concerned. Even though the actual marriage will be happening in Shahjahanabad. I have seen the palanquin that the Rajkumari will travel in. There are so many flowers, you can barely see the palanquin."

Most young girls welled up at the mere mention of a flower adorned palanquin. After all, the palanquin represented the fact that the girl would soon go away to her husband's home, leaving everything behind.

Well aware that the feeling would be so much more unbearable in Charumati's case, the younger daasi searched her face for a reaction. She was the daughter of Man Singh's dai and had always lived in one of the outhouses around the palace. She was only slightly older than the Princess and they had grown up playing *pithoo* and *sitholiya* together. Even back then, Bela had been envious of the young Charumati's quick movements and hand-eye coordination, which made her a master at both games. That jealousy intensified over the years when Bela realized the glaring disparities between them. While Charumati was constantly decked in the finest clothes and jewels, Bela had had to make do with hand-me-downs from the palace. While Charumati had a fleet of people waiting on her hand and foot, Bela's mother had started boasting to her friends that her seven-year-old daughter made the best *bajra rotis* in Kishengarh. Then came a day when Bela simply couldn't refute the differences that separated their worlds. She still vividly remembered the details. Bela wasn't in the mood to play. A stomach ache had kept her awake through the night and she'd only just dozed off when word came from the palace that the Princess wanted to play pithoo and needed company. Despite Bela's ardent protests that she wasn't up to it, her mother had forced her to put on her best clothes and go play with the Princess.

"It is not a choice, it is a command," she'd said in no uncertain terms.

"But I thought to play or not is always a choice." Bela had looked at her sulkily.

"Not for us," her mother had clarified then. "Choices are for people who can afford them. Now go! You must not keep the Princess waiting."

The gap kept deepening and then finally, the time came when Bela's mother told her that she was now being entrusted with the job of being the Rajkumari's personal daasi. "It is a huge honour for you, Bela. You will be responsible for Rajkumari sa's wardrobe, her royal chambers and her personal care and grooming. Make sure you do us proud. Our family has served the royal *khandaan* for generations."

Now, Bela smiled inwardly. Well, her mother had certainly been wrong about one thing. Speaking about choices, it was clear that Charumati's luck had run out. She might have had the freedom to take her own decisions before this, but it was evident that she had no choice at all as far as the most important decision of her life was concerned. Her marriage.

Kneeling down in front of the Princess, Bela tilted her head to one side. "Fret not, Rajkumari sa. I understand your predicament. This is not what any of us had imagined for you. But you have to make your peace with it. There is no other choice, is there?" She made a commiserating sound and looked at the Princess innocently.

"Bela!" the older maid stared at her sternly. "You must not forget what that oracle had said about Hukum. That she will marry a mighty and powerful ruler and that even though she will not be his first queen, she will most certainly be her husband's most favoured. We all know that the emperor's favourite wife passed away two years ago. I am sure Hukum will soon win his heart."

"But to win a heart, there has to be one too. It is often said about the emperor that he does not have a heart. Somebody who can imprison his own father and even restrict his food to a single dish, surely has no love for anyone in the world. Although his father did manage to outsmart him by choosing chickpeas, knowing that they can be prepared in a multitude of delicious recipes.[66] The father and the *khansama* turned out smarter than he had bargained for." Bela smirked.

In her excitement, she did not notice the shocked expression of the older maid, nor the disapproval on Nirmal's face. Only the Princess hadn't reacted.

"You talk too much, Bela." The other maid swatted her lightly on the hand. "Mark my words. Rajkumari sa's beauty and charm can melt the most austere of hearts. She will soon become the padshah begum of the shahi harem and then the emperor's daughter, Zeb-un-Nissa will have to regret her own actions. She was the one who instigated him against her. When she loses her position of supremacy in the harem, she will realize that she has dug her own grave."

"Yes, she needs to learn a lesson for sure. As does that old crone who had brought the paintings here in the first place. I cannot help but feel distressed at how easily she broke the promise she had made to Nirmal sa. Shameful to say the least!"

"That is enough," interrupted Nirmal suddenly. "You should know better than to give your opinion without being asked, Bela."

Bela clapped a hand over her mouth. "I am so sorry. I spoke too much. Please do not tell the Raja. I was just trying to express my love for the Princess and..."

"Ekant!" Nirmal's clear voice reverberated around the royal chamber. "You may go now. Both of you. Leave the clothes and jewellery here. I will help the Princess myself."

Leaving the thaalis behind, the two daasis scurried out of the room. Even as they shut the heavy brass door behind them, nobody noticed the knowing smile on Bela's face. Yes, everybody knew that the old woman had made a promise to Nirmal and hadn't kept it. But nobody was aware of the fact that she might have actually honoured the commitment had she not run into Bela outside the palace. Bela, who had been present in the courtyard and had witnessed the entire incident, had finally seen an outlet for the resentment she had harboured in her heart all her life.

"Wait!" It was merely a whisper, but the urgency in Bela's tone had stopped the woman in her tracks. After quickly looking around to make sure nobody was watching, Bela had dragged the woman behind a step-well.

"I already gave my word that I will not tell anyone," the protesting woman had said. She wrung her hands together. "Please trust me. I already...."

"Listen!" Bela caught the woman's bony hands and brought her face closer to hers. "Imagine what will happen to you if the emperor finds out from someone else. How furious he will be when he discovers that you knew and kept quiet. Why should you pay the price for the Rajkumari's mistake? A mistake that she does not even have any remorse for."

At that point, the woman had stopped and stared at Bela for a few moments, a frown on her wrinkled face as she tried to work out the purpose behind Bela's words.

"We are only servants," Bela had glanced in the direction of the palace and shaken her head. "*Yeh raaj gharane wale!* They think nothing of throwing us into the dungeons. Rest assured, if the emperor finds out that you were witness to this blasphemy and yet you kept quiet, you will never be heard of again." The palpable fear in the woman's eyes had boosted Bela's confidence, "On the other hand, you will most definitely be handsomely rewarded if you...."

She had left the sentence unfinished, but the message was as clear as day. Having accomplished what she had meant to, Bela released the woman's hands, covered her face with her odhni and then as fast as she could, ran back into the palace. Even as she watched her go, the old woman suddenly realized that she didn't even know the girl's name. But what did it matter? She was just a poor man's daughter, a lowly girl who didn't have the good fortune to make her own choices, yet had managed to wield enough power to ensure the downfall of the Princess of Kishengarh.

CHAPTER 12

Rana Raj Singh was well aware of the fact that at the moment, the Mughals were in a numerically superior position. That meant that an open encounter was out of the question and the only viable option was an ambush. This was something that the Rana was adept at. After all, it was his great-great-grandfather, Maharana Pratap, who had first used guerilla warfare against the Mughals in India. By the time the Maharana's accession to the throne happened in 1572, Chittor had already been lost to Akbar. However, most of the wooded and hilly region was still under the Sisodia rule and Akbar had to approach Pratap for a treaty since he wanted to establish a safe route to Gujarat via Mewar. Pratap, in the true Sisodia spirit, repeatedly rejected Akbar's proposal, ultimately leading to the Battle of Haldighati. Following the battle, Akbar failed to capture the Maharana and his closest aides. Instead of surrendering to Mughal administration, Pratap hid in the hilly areas near Chittor and plotted *dhar*, a form of guerilla warfare. He had by then understood the disadvantages of open wars and long sieges. The long-term planning and enormous resources that were needed for war was one thing, but it was also the colossal loss of human life that was inevitable in open battles that made him think of an alternative. Dhar on the other hand, if carried out tactically, had a much better chance of weakening an otherwise larger and stronger enemy. Pratap would discreetly hit Mughal camps, supply columns or weak outposts, and this quickly became one of his prime strategies. He also realized the importance of operating amidst a friendly rather than hostile population. Supportive locals could greatly increase their chances of winning by providing assistance in the form of shelter, supplies, information and even recruits. Pratap made it his business to befriend the locals, granted them *jaghirs* to solidify their loyalty, and made the most inaccessible and impenetrable parts of the Aravali hills, his abode. He, in fact, never stayed for long in one place. Instead, he kept moving, making it difficult for his adversary to trace him.[67]

"It is the only way to cripple the enemy right in the beginning," Rana Raj Singh said to Manik Lal now as they rode through the forest together. Word had already been sent to Udaipur and the Rana's best force had been summoned. "We will choose a hilly spot on the route from Kishengarh to Shahjahanabad. A narrow pass preferably. You will help us find one, considering that you know these ways so well."

"I can do more than that, Rana ji." Manik Lal was riding a little ahead of the Rana since he knew the shortest route out of the forest. Now as he turned his head to look at Raj Singh, he couldn't help thinking what an imposing figure the Rana made on his horse. With his ramrod posture, barrel chest and handlebar moustache, he looked every bit the proud ruler of Mewar. Manik Lal was just grateful that he'd been given a chance to prove his loyalty.

"I can disguise myself as a Mughal and join the enemy. Then, while you and your men are keeping them occupied, I will take the Princess and hide her in a safe spot."

"It is a very dangerous thing to do. If you get caught and they discover that you are an imposter, they will most certainly kill you."

"Do not worry about that, Rana ji. I speak the language and know their customs very well. I take full responsibility that no harm will come to the Princess. I will guard her with my life until you defeat the enemy and come for her."

"You seem to be very sure of that," remarked the Rana.

"Of your victory?" Manik Lal smiled at the man who had, in a matter of a few minutes, won his respect. "I have no qualms about that at all."

"Do not forget that we are a very small contingent compared to them."

Manik Lal stopped his horse. "Thirty-two forts to defend Mewar," he said. "Defeated the combined armies of Sultan Mahmud Khilji of Malwa and the ruler of Gujarat and commemorated his victory by constructing the Vijay Stambha."

Raj Singh looked at Manik Lal quizzically. "You are no doubt talking about the great Rana Kumba. But what are you trying to say?"

Manik Lal smiled. "Eighty wounds, one arm, one leg. One hundred battles and he only lost once."

"Rana Sanga, of course."

"Seven feet five inches tall. Famed for carrying an eighty-kilogram spear and wearing an armour weighing seventy-two kilos. He never conceded to Mughal rule, yet won the respect and admiration of Akbar. Ultimately managed to recover most of Mewar."

Now Raj Singh smiled back at Manik Lal. "The greatest warrior of them all, Maharana Pratap Singh Sisodia."

Manik Lal nodded. "You hail from that lineage, Rana ji. That is your bloodline. You will take the Princess back to Udaipur with you. Of that, I am as certain as I am of the fact that the sun will rise tomorrow."

***

The verdant Aravali hills and tranquil waters of Lake Gundalao had not been a witness to a celebration like this in a very long time. In fact, by the sound of the festivities that were going on inside the palace, anyone would have thought that the entire kingdom was rejoicing. The general feeling of melancholy that the majority of its inhabitants had been experiencing for days had been adequately masked for the benefit of the baraat. Now, the music and *naach* that was an integral part of all Rajput weddings had been going on for hours in the palace with the *ghoomar* being the most popular. The delicate hand movements, dazzling lehengas worn by the twirling women and flawless synchronization, were a spectacular sight to watch. First performed by women from the Bhil tribes in reverence to Goddess Saraswati, the name 'ghoomar' was literally derived from the word 'ghoomna' or going around in circles. The Rajputs who were in constant conflict with the Bhils, adopted this particularly graceful dance form when they defeated the tribe and embraced many of their practices. Ghoomar then entered the royal courts and zenanas of the Rajputs, and women started performing the dance on special occasions such as coronations, incoming of monsoon, festivals like Teej, and weddings. Now so many years later, no Rajput wedding was conducted without this auspicious dance form.

While the revelries were on in full swing in the courtyards and gardens, an army of cooks toiled in the *shahi rasoi*, preparing elaborate meals for the baraat. There was a separate lineup of *halwais* who were hard at work packing box after box of sweetmeats which would be presented to the baraatis just before the *vidaai*. It was customary for the wedding parties to exchange gifts and the baraat had arrived laden with clothes and jewellery for the bride along with hundreds of boxes of sweetmeats covered with *chandi ka varq*. Originating in Persia, this tradition of gilding food with thin silver sheets, had been perfected by the Mughals in India. The silversmiths who pounded the silver into sheets by hand, worked with the utmost precision and every sheet was 1/8000 of a millimetre thin. Varq was a part of Mughal palace life, a sign of royalty. The Rajputs, of course, were not to be outdone, and the *shagun* boxes containing the mouthwatering *ghewar* and *choorma* ladoos that the region was famed for, now occupied one entire section of the kitchen. Two men had been assigned exclusively to count and seal the boxes. There could be no error. Not a single baraati could return empty-handed.

Meanwhile, the atmosphere in the women's chambers was far from celebratory. The haldi had taken place the previous day and then Charumati had gone to the Kuldevi temple for the puja early that morning. Most people who saw her wondered about her state of mind. Anger, regret, resignation? It was difficult to gauge her mood. After returning to the palace, she had gone straight to her room and stayed there. In the meantime, the other members of the zenana continued with the preparations, but there was a palpable pall of gloom that hung heavy in the air.

"This is most certainly the first time that I am grateful for the seclusion," remarked Nirmal to Charumati's paternal aunt. They were sitting side-by-side on the hand painted rosewood couch in Nirmal's bedroom. Charumati's trunks were packed and ready, and her aunt was checking to see that nothing had been forgotten. "At least here, we do not have to disguise our true feelings behind a veneer of pretence."

"Nirmal, do not speak so loudly." The older woman placed a finger to her lips. "*Deewaro ke bhi kaan hote hain.*"

"Well, this is the worst that can happen, is it not?" Nirmal shrugged. Then she looked thoughtful. "You know, *Tai sa,* I have had the strangest feeling since the morning."

She frowned, as if trying to work out her thoughts. "As though, despite what we think is inevitable, it might not actually be so."

The lady looked baffled. "What are you trying to say, Nirmal? Charu's fate is sealed. The baraat is here, two thousand of them! Charu's hands have been adorned with *mehndi*. The palanquin decorated with flowers awaits her."

"The palanquin!" Nirmal's face suddenly lit up, a glimmer of clarity in her eyes. "It is the palanquin!"

"Nirmal, please do not speak in riddles."

Nirmal shifted closer to the older woman. "Tai sa, I could not sleep last night. At about five o'clock in the morning, I went for a walk around the palace. That is when I happened to see the palanquin."

"And?"

"In the beginning, even as I stood there looking at it, I felt a sense of distress. It was *this* palanquin that was destined to carry Charu to Shahjahanabad, to her worst fate. So much so that I had a desire to actually hurl it off the nearest hill. As if by getting rid of it, all Charu's problems will be solved. But then..."

Charumati's aunt looked at her quizzically. "Then what?"

Nirmal took a deep breath. "Then all of a sudden, that feeling changed. It was almost as though the palanquin was speaking to me. Telling me that it has other plans, a different purpose. That its final destination is not Shahjahanabad, but somewhere else. That something better, much better lies in wait for our Charu."

"Are you sure you were not asleep in your bed and dreaming, Nirmal?" The woman shook her head sadly. "We have all made our peace with the fact that Charu is fated to be Aurangzeb's wife. It is better if Charu and you also accept the inevitable. Dreaming, wishing, hoping will simply not help. It will, on the contrary, make Charu's vidaai even more difficult for all of us. It is a mercy that her father is not alive. This would have been a very difficult day for him."

Nirmal didn't say any more. Instead, she got up from the couch and, crossing the bedroom, walked toward one of the many jaali windows in her sitting area. Even as she looked down now, she could clearly see the palanquin. She stared at it for a few minutes. It seemed to stare back at her.

No, this one was definitely not going to Shahjahanabad.

Nirmal almost wanted to cry out with joy. The Rana was on his way. She knew it with the utmost certainty. She could feel it in her bones.

There was another reason for the enormous sense of relief she suddenly felt. When that girl Bela and the other daasi had been talking yesterday, they'd mentioned the oracle.

That oracle was famed for her accuracy. People from all over the region went to her. She was a blind woman who lived on her own, in the wilderness. Noblemen and commoners alike would go to her and ask her to predict their future. Her abode was under a banyan tree, and she kept an enormous earthen pot of water in front of her. She would then ask the person to throw some coins or jewels into the pot based on their means. As soon as that was done, images would form in the water. These were distorted images which only she could understand. Payment was always based on what a particular person could afford, but that did not affect the precision with which her predictions unfailingly came true.

The older daasi had said that when the oracle had predicted Charu's future, she had stated that Charu would marry a mighty king and that even though she would not be his first queen, she would be his most favoured. And nobody could deny that Aurangzeb was mighty. And that despite the current circumstances, Charu might indeed win him over with her beauty and charm and become his most favoured.

Nirmal smiled to herself. There was one other thing that the oracle had said, which everyone seemed to have forgotten. She had clearly stated that Charu would marry a man who she loved dearly.

And there was only one man in the world who Charumati loved. Rana Raj Singh.

Nirmal glanced at the palanquin again. "Now I know where you are headed," she whispered softly. "Your destination is not Shahjahanabad. It is Udaipur."

Then, with a laugh, Nirmal skipped to the other side of the room and flung open the balcony door. Instantly, the sounds of dhol and shehnai wafted in from the ghoomar being performed in the main courtyard below. Taking Charumati's aunt by the hand, Nirmal pulled her up to her feet. Protesting, the surprised woman tried to stop her. "Nirmal *chhori!* What are you doing? No, no...."

But Nirmal waved her protests away and within moments, the two of them were dancing on the balcony, moving in perfectly symmetrical circles, clapping their hands and snapping their fingers. The older woman was simply dancing, her body naturally responding to the mesmerizing music that she'd listened to all her life. But Nirmal wasn't simply dancing. Nirmal was celebrating, rejoicing, revelling in the jubilant realization that her best friend's destiny might indeed be where her true happiness lay.

CHAPTER 13

Even as a child, Charumati had been lovely. With her long lustrous hair, ebony eyes, luminous skin and radiant smile, she was easily one of the prettiest girls in Kishengarh. That was the age, the growing up phase when most girls displayed a certain awkwardness, a hesitation about themselves. Charu, on the other hand, possessed confident elegance, a dignity that was rare to see among such young girls. Then, as she grew older, it became evident that she was more than just elegant. People all around the region started talking about her stunning beauty and irresistible charm.

"She really does look exquisite in anything she wears," remarked a family friend who was visiting the palace one day.

"Yes, there will be no dearth of proposals for her," agreed Charumati's aunt then. "The best of princes and kings will line up to marry her. Speaking of which, I cannot wait to see her on her wedding day. This is a woman whose beauty cannot be concealed even in that plain white churidar and kurta that she dons for her talwar baazi lessons. Can you imagine how enchanting she will look in her wedding poshak?"

Now, dressed in the rani pink lehenga choli with the heavily embellished odhni that effectively veiled the upper part of her face as per tradition, the Princess did look spectacular. The kundan and polki jewellery that she wore had belonged to her grandmother, and the women in the zenana gasped when they saw it, remarking in stunned tones that it seemed to weigh almost as much as the Princess herself. Charumati had admired the jewellery ever since she'd been a little girl, but today, she'd put it on with a very heavy heart. Despite the ghoonghat, it was hard not to notice the big dark eyes that were now misty with the tears that refused to leave their abode.

"You are a Rajput, daughter. Your heart might be breaking but you may never allow the world to see your tears." It was almost as though her father was there, she could feel his presence so palpably.

"*Nazar na lage.*" Nirmal's voice snapped the Princess out of her thoughts, and she turned around to look at her friend. She was helping her to get ready for the impending vidaai and they were alone in Charu's bedroom.

Nirmal picked up a pot of kajal from the dressing table. Dipping her finger into it, she then smeared a tiny bit behind her friend's ear. It was common practice to mark a *kaala tikka* on a bride's forehead or behind the ear. "This is even more important if the bride is as beautiful as you are, Charu," said Nirmal. "In fact, undoubtedly the most resplendent bride I have ever seen. And I have seen quite a few."

Finally, she took two pairs of jootis from the cupboard and held them up for Charu to inspect.

"Gold or pink?"

"Perhaps neither." Charumati shook her head.

"What do you mean?" Nirmal looked confused.

"Well, I daresay the emperor will be pleased to see me arrive barefoot. After all, it was my jooti that crushed his painting into a million smithereens, was it not? He will think I am truly repenting my actions." Charumati smiled sadly. "Do not worry, dear friend. I am joking. I thought I would have a last laugh with you before I leave."

Wiping her eyes, Nirmal placed the gold jootis in front of her friend. "These are softer. I know you will be comfortable in the palanquin, but still. It is a long way to Shahjahanabad."

"Shahjahanabad?" Charumati scoffed. "You really think I will wait that long?"

Lowering her voice, she pointed to her neck. There, nestled between the heavy kundan choker and *rani haar,* was a thin gold chain with a tiny pendant hanging from its end. The pendant was the sort that opened up from one side.

"Snake poison." Charumati nodded. "I told you earlier, did I not? The Badshah can take me, but he shall not have me. I will consume this before we enter the gates of Shahjahanabad."

Nirmal pulled her friend into her arms. Even as they hugged one last time, she brought her lips close to Charumati's ears and whispered softly, so softly that even the Princess could barely make out the words. "Throw that chain away, Charu, for you will not need it. We may not have heard anything yet, but I know it in my heart. The Rana is on his way."

Pulling back, she held her hand out for the chain.

"But Nirmal, what if he does not make it in time? What if..."

"If you truly love him, if you believe in him, then you will abandon all misgivings, all uncertainties, Charu. Have faith in him and give that chain to me now."

Without a word, Charumati took the chain off and handed it to Nirmal.

The sound of running feet outside alerted both the girls. A minute later, there was a knock at the door. "Rajkumari sa! May I come in?"

The voice was Bela's. Nirmal looked heavenwards. "I do not understand how you can even bear her, Charu. She has such a sly, watchful look about her."

"She is not a bad sort, poor girl. You have disliked her since she beat you at pithoo all those years ago." Smoothening down her lehenga, Charumati called Bela into the room.

The young daasi stepped in. Folding her hands reverently, she said, "Raja Man Singh has sent me, Rajkumari sa. It is almost time for the vidaai. The baraatis would like to cross the rocky, hilly terrain ahead of the fort before it gets dark. Hence, they would like to leave soon."

"Thank you, Bela." Nirmal stepped forward. "I will bring the Princess down. You can leave now."

Bela smirked to herself. That Nirmal had always been overprotective of the Princess, but these days she was practically guarding her! She was constantly in the princess's room, the two of them huddled together, whispering to each other. Well, it wasn't going to last long, was it? Soon, very soon the Princess would bid goodbye to her precious best friend and then she would be gone forever from Kishengarh.

The daasi turned to bow to the Princess one last time. As she lowered her head, she couldn't help remembering her mother's words the previous night. "Oh Bela, I cannot believe that the Princess will go away tomorrow. How much you will miss her when she leaves! You have been taking care of her for so many years."

'Yes Ma. And I have carried out my final duties toward her with the utmost sincerity as well,' thought Bela to herself as she left the princess's bedroom and closed the door.

***

The sun hung low on the horizon, not quite ready to retire for the day. The time that had been predicted for sunset had passed half an hour ago, but it seemed as though just like the rest of Kishengarh, the sun too, was in a mood to prolong the inevitable.

The Rajputs and the Mughals had congregated at the entrance of the fort. Family and senior members of the court were in front, while the staff was at the back. A normal vidaai would have had the bride's parents escort the newly married couple to the flower decked gates. The bride's mother would have held a silver *thaal* filled with rice, and the bride would take handfuls and toss it over her head. She would do this five times without looking back and her father would be standing behind her, waiting to catch the grains in the drape of his pagadi. This ceremony was symbolic of the girl leaving her home to start her married life in her husband's house. Then the bride's parents would bless the newlyweds and escort their daughter to the waiting palanquin.

The flower decked palanquin awaited Charumati, but in every other way, this vidaai was different. While most brides were sad at the thought of leaving their homes and going away, they usually smiled through their tears with much to look forward to. Charumati, on the other hand, could barely stop the tears now as she made her way to the palanquin. She clutched Nirmal's hand tightly, digging her long fingernails into her friend's palm. For the first time in her life, Nirmal could see something resembling fear in the eyes of this valiant Rajput Princess. Leaning over, she whispered in the princess's ears, reiterating what she had said before.

"He is on his way, Charu. You have to have faith. If not in that oracle's words, if not even in your best friend's instinct, then at least in the Rana. How can you imagine he will ever let you down?"

"*Bhavani Ma ki sau,* if he does not come, I will kill myself. You may have taken the poison away, but this earth is like a mother to me. I know she will gladly open her arms for this daughter of hers. I will jump from one of these mountains and end my life rather than enter the gates of Shahjahanabad. Goodbye, Nirmal."

The Princess squeezed her friend's hand for the last time and then, as though resigning herself to whatever fate had in store, walked forward to step into the palanquin. Man Singh and she had already exchanged a tearful farewell earlier that day. He had thought his sister wouldn't even look at him and she might not have, but the grief of separation overpowered any anger that she had felt toward him. Now, the sound of the shehnai grew louder as final goodbyes were exchanged between the Rajputs and the Mughals. A small Rajput contingent consisting of a few horsemen would accompany the Princess on her journey, along with several daasis who had been assigned to her personal service once she reached Shahjahanabad.

The palanquin was lifted off the ground by four burly men and a generous shower of rose petals sprinkled on it. It was going to be a long journey and inside the palanquin, the princess's mind was a troubled labyrinth of misgivings, hopes, and fears. A hundred questions raced through her mind as she turned back to look at Kishengarh Fort for the very last time. Other than the fact that it had been her home until now, Charumati had always loved the beauty and majesty of the fort, with its imposing columns, grand walls, and turrets that rose high above the glistening waters of the surrounding lake.

"Your taste in architecture is beautiful, baba," Charumati had often told her father. He had also been an ardent patron of the arts and during his reign, the fort palace had become the centre of local art and music.

"So many happy memories," sighed the Princess to herself as she craned her neck to catch a few final glimpses. Now, of course, she could hardly see anything of the pale white stone for the entire front of the structure had been draped with marigold garlands. Despite the grandeur of the decoration, to Charumati's eyes, it was a melancholic sight. As though the fort too was inwardly weeping, mourning along with its inhabitants.

The palanquin turned a corner, and the fort disappeared from sight. The contingent moved slowly at that point since the road ahead was steep and they were going downhill. The curtains draped around the opening of the palanquin were made of sheer fabric to let in some sunlight. Through the transparent material, Charumati could look outside and she suddenly spotted a horseman coming from the opposite direction. He was on his way to the fort and was galloping along at a fine pace, so all the Princess got was a fleeting look. It was, however, enough for her to ascertain that he was the man she'd despatched to Udaipur with a message for the Rana. Her trusted messenger! An instant desperation took over Charumati's senses, and she had to clap a hand over her mouth to restrain herself from calling out to him as he came nearer. His face was in profile, but the Princess strained her eyes for some indication, some sign, of whether he had been able to deliver the message or not. Had he reached in time? Had the Rana been there? What had he said? Was he on his way right now?

Charumati wanted to wrench open the curtains and try to catch the man's eye, but she didn't dare. If the horseman had managed to reach Udaipur in time and meet the Rana, the last thing she wanted to do was jeopardise the Rana's chances of getting to her. The horseman must have also noticed the passing contingent, it was hard to miss, but he didn't let anything on. On the contrary, he didn't even glance her way, and his expression gave nothing away as he rode past the palanquin.

The Princess leaned back against the cushions and closed her eyes.

I send letters to my Beloved,
The dear Krishna.
But He sends no message of reply,
Purposely preserving silence.

Unconsciously, the first words of a poem by Mirabai had come to her lips. She'd first read the poem as a child, and she'd liked the play of words very much. She had however, been too young to fully comprehend the depth of the yearning. Now she strained to recall the rest of it and as it slowly came back to her, her lips started moving in recitation.

I sweep his path in readiness
And gaze and gaze
Till my eyes turn blood-shot.
I have no peace by night or day.

My heart is fit to break.
O my Master, You were my companion
In former births.
When will you come?

A hundred and fifty years separated her from this woman, this mystic poet who had lived solely for the deep love that she felt for her one and only. Yet Mirabai was like a kindred spirit. Her pain, her desire, her longing was so familiar that it almost felt like it belonged to her. A mirror reflection of her own.

"When will you come? When will you come?"

Her eyes still tightly shut, Charumati clutched a hand to her chest and repeated the last words of the poem to herself. The hills and forests rolled by as the palanquin picked up speed. A caravan of camels overtook the passing contingent, their humped backs piled high with merchandise. In the west, somewhere behind the rolling sand dunes, the sun could be seen slowly making its way down, its last rays like vermillion on a deep blue horizon. Charumati, though, noticed nothing. She just kept murmuring the words again and again, over and over, so softly that even she could barely hear herself... when will you come, when will you come, when will you come?

CHAPTER 14

Positioning and location. The two decisions that need to be taken with utmost care when planning dhar.

Generations of Rajputs had learnt and imbibed this lesson from their forefathers. After all, some of the greatest battles had been fought and won not in the open battlefields but by this strategic military tactic. A military tactic that went all the way back to the ancient times, when it had first been used in the sixth century. The Chinese, the Persians, the Romans, even the Celtic, Germanic and African tribes had used it to successfully ward off and defeat an otherwise formidable enemy. Then the medieval empires had adopted the technique and Maharana Pratap had been the first Indian king to use it in an organized form in the subcontinent.[68] Later the Jats, Sikhs and Marathas employed it and Shivaji Raje in fact, implemented his own version of guerilla warfare called *Shiva Sutra* or *Gamini Kava* and established the Maratha state in 1674. The Rajputs had by then, mastered dhar to perfection.

Now the Rana's force was positioned on both sides of the hills that surrounded the road from Kishengarh to Shahjahanabad. The lush teak and bamboo trees that grew in these parts in abundance provided a perfect cover and thick, strong ropes had been tied from one rocky edge to another. These would be used by the men for support before they landed on the road. The pots were in place and had been secured with trip wires. The archers were the kind who were known for never missing a target.

It was the steadfast Manik Lal who had successfully led the Rana's men to this particular rocky spot in the slopes. The Rana understood how well accustomed Manik Lal was to the hills and forests in this area, and he was grateful to have the former dacoit by his side. The ravine that separated the hills was steep and narrow and the Rana knew that the Mughals would need to go past it with caution, particularly considering the size of their contingent. The nifty informer he had sent to Kishengarh had also managed to find out the exact time that the Mughals had departed, and the fact that they were being led by one of Aurangzeb's trusted generals, the valiant Mubarak Khan.

"The width of the ravine will work to our advantage, Hukum."

The archer who had spoken did not turn to look at the Rana. He had been trained to never take his eyes off the target. "And of course, they have been on the road for more than fifteen hours, so some amount of exhaustion is to be expected. It will most certainly be a slow-moving contingent. That will give us enough time to ensure maximum damage."

"Well, it is obvious that there is no room for even a single miscalculation. After all, we are fifty, while there are two thousand of them." Rana Raj Singh's brow was furrowed, not with worry, but with concentration. "Though, there is one obvious advantage that we have over them."

"What, Hukum?" Manik Lal asked with interest. They had already discussed the strategy in the minutest of details.

"*Yeh dharti!*" Bending down, Raj Singh took a handful of soil in his right hand and held it out for everyone to see. "Yeh dharti; it is our homeland, our legacy, our birthright. Our forefathers died protecting it. This earth will not let us down, of that I am very sure."

He smeared the soil on his forehead and one by one, all the men did the same.

Aware that his force was now well motivated and sure of themselves, the Rana turned back to Manik Lal. He and three other men had disguised themselves as Mughals. It was the four of them who had been placed with the responsibility of carrying the princess's palanquin to safety once the battle started. "You were right about this disguise," said the Rana. "You have managed to pull it off very well, too well, in fact. Despite knowing otherwise, it is difficult even for me to believe that the four of you are actually Rajputs."

Manik Lal laughed. "Well then, it is a good thing that there are only fifty of us and every man here is well aware of my reality. Otherwise, a terrible error could occur."

The Rana shook his head. "Like I said before, there is no place for miscalculations or errors in the implementation of our strategy. Though there is one thing that I feel the need to reiterate to you, Manik Lal."

"Ji Hukum?"

"I want the Princess out of the line of fire. If she steps out of the palanquin, it will become difficult to separate her from the chaos."

"Princess Charumati is a Rajput and is well versed in a situation like this. I am sure she will remain in the palanquin. We will then take her to safety. I have already identified the perfect spot. There is a cave on the other side of that hill where I will hide her. Do not worry, Hukum. I will guard her with my life."

Suddenly, a sharp trilling broke through the stillness of the hills. It was a shrill sound, like one that a small bird might make. The first trill was quickly followed by several more, all at different intervals.

The sounds appeared to be coming from different parts of the hills, as though it was not one, but many birds who were making them. Only the fifty men hiding in their predetermined spots knew that it wasn't the birds, it was one of them who had made the sounds. The man in question was in fact not a part of the Rana's military at all. He was a ventriloquist, adept at the skill of voice illusion. A member of Udaipur's most famed Kathputli troop, he had been hired especially for this mission.

"The signal," murmured the Rana, as the seventh call went out and echoed off the hills. His face had taken on a tenor of intense concentration. "Here they come."

The turn between the mountains was a steep one and several of the men in hiding had a bird's-eye view from their chosen spots. The Mughal contingent came into sight and, as expected, it was moving at a deliberately unhurried pace. It was evident that many of them were not used to this undulating, rocky terrain and were moving with caution. First came the men on foot, their swords neatly stuck by the sides of their uniforms. They were closely followed by men on horses and considering the restricted width of the road, they'd had to even out into pairs. The princess's palanquin was in the centre, secured from both front and back.

A final call went off, and the Rana saw that the contingent was now perfectly positioned on the road. Without a moment's hesitation, the designated archer took aim. Four arrows in a quick succession of each other pierced through the pots. The contents were viscous, the consistency almost like that of an adhesive and the Rana watched grimly, as the pots broke one by one, and the liquid poured out. Every man in the Rana's force checked to make sure that his face gear was in place. Then, not wasting a single second, the archer took aim again. This time, his target was the fifth and final pot that had been placed higher than the others. Once again, the arrow pierced through with perfect precision. A low, ominous humming instantly filled the air.

"*Jai Bhavani!*"

"Jai Bhavani!"

"Jai Bhavani!"

The roars reverberated around the hills as all fifty men drew their swords and plunged down. The Rana had chosen his men with care and each one was thoroughly adept. It was a quick, smooth descent and as soon as their feet touched the ground, the men used their pocket knives to cut the ropes that had secured them.

The bees, of course, hadn't wasted a single moment. Instantly drawn to the sticky liquid that had fallen on the unsuspecting contingent, they now swarmed around them relentlessly, stinging them wherever they could. As a result, several of the men panicked and fell off the ravine while others tried their best to ward off the stings.

"Where did they come from?" shouted one man to another. "I did not see any bee hives here! And that liquid! How did it...."

Suddenly, seemingly from thin air, a burly Rajput appeared right in front of him. His face was protected by the armour he wore, and he held a shield in one hand and a sword in the other. The sword he wielded had been polished to perfection, so much so that the enemy could clearly see his reflection in it.

"Ambush! Ambush! It is an ambush!"

Those were his last words before the glistening sword was raised and plunged through his body. The man drew a raspy last breath and stumbled to the ground.

And then it seemed as though the same scene was repeated over and over again, as the Rajputs began to strike. The Mughals, too stunned by the bee attack, were simply not prepared to defend themselves, let alone strike back. Bitten and injured, they continued to fall down the sides of the ravine while Raj Singh's men pursued the rest.

Meanwhile, Charumati, still sitting in the palanquin, didn't need to be told what was going on. She'd heard the repetitive war cries of 'Jai Bhavani' and even though her heart was thumping with anxiety at the commotion outside, the despair she had been feeling earlier had dissipated.

All was not lost. The Rana was here! He had not let her down after all!

She had absolutely no idea how many men he had brought with him, how prepared they were to face a contingent of two thousand Mughals, and whether they even had a strategy or not. Yet, just knowing that the Rana was here, that he truly loved her and had come at her bidding, was enough to make her heart sing with joy.

Suddenly, she felt the palanquin being hastily lifted off the ground by four men. Even as they balanced the vehicle, turned and hurried off in the opposite direction, the Princess gripped the railings tightly on both sides. Who was it? The Rajputs taking her to safety? The Mughals trying to hide her somewhere while the battle was on? Or worse still, dacoits? Terrified, Charumati tried to quiet her thumping heart and strained her eyes to look outside. The curtains were still drawn and all she could make out were the figures of men fighting valiantly. The colours of the uniforms were different, but it was difficult to tell much else and nearly impossible to accurately identify anyone. Though Charumati would have known right away if the Rana had appeared. She didn't need eyes to recognize him. Her heart would have told her instantly.

It took several minutes for Manik Lal and the others to navigate their way between the fighting men and carry the palanquin toward the cave. To Charumati, though, it felt like hours as she imagined the worst scenarios. The apprehension she felt and the shaky movement of the vehicle made her feel nauseous, and she was almost ready to pass out by the time the palanquin was finally placed on the sandy floor of the cave. Too numb with fear at what might happen next, the Princess didn't dare to move. She did observe that it was now completely dark outside, and no light filtered in through the thin drapes. The temperature also seemed to have suddenly dropped. The war cries sounded more muffled, as though they were coming from afar. Here, wherever they were, the chaos had quietened considerably.

With shaking hands, the Princess drew open the drapes. Covering her face with the ghoonghat, she gathered the voluminous skirt of her ghagra and tentatively stepped out of the palanquin.

"Careful, Rajkumari sa! Please mind your head."

Heeding the well-timed warning, the Princess bent her head and looked around. It was too dark to see clearly, but from the rocky walls and sandy floor around her, she could make out that they were in a cave. Deeper inside, the sound of dripping water could be heard. The shadowy figures of four burly men were silhouetted against the thin sunbeam that was flickering in from the cave's entrance. Despite the lack of light, Charumati was able to decipher from their dark-coloured uniforms and armour that they were Mughal soldiers.

"Are you all right, Rajkumari sa? Do you need anything? Water perhaps?"

Charumati stared at the soldier who had spoken. By the look of his clothes and appearance, he was most certainly a Mughal. His manner of speaking and dialect, however, was that of a Rajput.

"We apologize for the clumsiness, but we were in a hurry to get you to safety."

"Who are you?" The suspicion in her eyes was palpable. "Why have you brought me here?"

Manik Lal could have kicked himself. He stepped forward and bowed. "I am so sorry, Hukum. I forgot about the disguise. Do not be afraid. We are Rana ji's men disguised to mislead the Mughals."

"Rana Raj Singh's men?"

"Ji, Hukum. Rana ji has placed us in charge of your safety. My name is Manik Lal."

Even though the man had no proof of what he was saying, Charumati was certain that he was speaking the truth. He had dead honest eyes. Taking a step toward him, she addressed him by his name.

"Where is the Rana, Manik Lal?" she asked anxiously. "Tell me quickly. Is he fine?"

"Yes. He is all right." Even as he said the words, Manik Lal sent a silent prayer to Bhawani Ma to protect the Rana. He had seen him fleetingly as he and the others were rushing with the palanquin. Surrounded by the enemy, he was fighting fearlessly, holding his own. But this kind of battle was as fast as it was unpredictable.

Trying to push his fears away, Manik Lal bowed to the Princess and proffered a copper container filled to the brim with crystal clear water. "You must be tired, Hukum. Here is some water. Please."

The Princess accepted the container and took several gulps.

"This water is fresh!" she exclaimed in surprise. "As though it has just been filled. How did you manage to get such fresh, cool water here?"

"I know every *baori* in these parts, Hukum," answered Manik Lal. "And while there is none as big and well known as the famed Chand Baori, most of them serve their purpose just as well."

Built in the ninth century in Abhaneri village by Raja Chanda of the Nikumbh dynasty, Chand Baori was the oldest, deepest and largest step-well in the region.[69] The geometric calculation of stairs and steps was done in a way that these baoris were able to provide a respite from the heat and guarantee water supply even in the arid months. Hardly acting merely as sources of water, the stepwells were also hubs of social, religious and cultural life.

Charumati smiled. "Well, there certainly cannot be a Chand Baori everywhere," she agreed. "But the water is just as delicious."

Once the Princess had had her fill, Manik Lal reached into the palanquin. Retrieving a few cushions and a *dohar*, he spread them out on a downy part of the cave's floor. Folding his hands, he bid Charumati to rest for a while. "Please do not worry. Bhairon Singh and I will be guarding the entrance of the cave with our lives." Charumati could see that Manik Lal's companion was as burly and strong as him.

"What about the other two?" she asked. "Will they be returning to the battle?"

"It would be the wise thing to do, Hukum. With only fifty of us fighting two thousand of them, we need every available man."

"Fifty! There are only fifty of you?" Charumati looked at Manik Lal in alarm.

"I am afraid so." Manik Lal nodded gravely.

"Then please hurry back. Do not waste a single instant. All of you go. I am perfectly all right on my own."

"It was my solemn promise to Rana ji that Bhairon Singh and I would stay to protect you. I cannot break the promise."

Charumati knew that arguing or debating would be of no use. A promise, a commitment made by a Rajput was set in stone. He would rather die than dishonour it. She watched with anxious eyes as the two other men picked up their swords and shields and rushed out. Manik Lal and Bhairon Singh took up their places outside, one on either side of the cave.

Fifty men valiantly fighting two thousand of the enemy! Fear and hopelessness tried to take over her senses, but Charumati resolutely drove it all away, trying to concentrate instead on her best friend's words. *Trust the Rana, Charu. Have faith in him. He will take you back to Udaipur.*

Udaipur. The crown of the Kingdom of Mewar. Echoes of a regal past seemed to resonate around the darkened cave, those majestic palaces, colossal walls and glorious forts. And the tales that they held within, tales of those lionhearted Rajputs who did not need an army. They were the army.

"Jai Bhavani! Jai Bhavani!"

Despite being muffled, the war cries outside grew more ferocious. Charumati closed her eyes, envisioning herself elsewhere, in another time, another place. The image grew vivid, more vivid, until she could see herself clearly, standing on one of the balconies of the *Dilkhush Mahal*, that mirrored palace of joy in Raj Mahal that had been made for the royal ladies by Raj Singh's grandfather, Maharana Karan Singh. She was looking down from the balcony at the shimmering waters of Lake Pichola, when she suddenly spotted him from a distance. Rana Raj Singh, entering the gates of the palace. He was sitting atop his horse, tall, regal, handsome. The ride uphill was an arduous one for most people, but Raj Singh rode on effortlessly through the enormous Badi Pol, all the way up the paved road to the first courtyard. Then, he got down from his horse, turned around and looked up at her. And as his face broadened into a smile, Charumati smiled back and whispered softly, "Thank you for coming, my love."

Chapter 15

It was a clear day in Shahjahanabad and the emperor had chosen to sit out in the greens directly in front of the Diwan-i-Aam. The gardeners had been hard at work that entire month and now the gardens looked like something out of a picture. But this was not surprising since gardens were a vital part of imperial living for the Mughal emperors since the time of Babur. People had initially planted gardens without much order or structure but after Babur came to power, gardens were methodically included in the structural plan of the palaces.[70] The neatly trimmed hedges, the mesmerizing aroma that emanated from the wide variety of trees, shrubs and flowers that were planted in abundance by skilled gardeners, and the tinkling of fountains that spouted crystal clear water or sometimes *golab*, ensured that the gardens were a consistently favourite spot among members of the royal household.

Now as he walked across the garden toward the emperor, Jai Singh chanced upon one of the younger eunuchs from Zeb-un-Nissa's palace. The eunuch was carrying a basket over one arm and was obviously there to pick flowers. Jai Singh frowned. He did not like this one. Always there at the slightest opportunity, forever ready to eavesdrop. Though not senior in rank, the eunuch was in immense awe of the Princess and fiercely loyal to her.

"Beautiful roses, are they not?"

Gesturing toward the nearest bed, the eunuch smiled coyly at the general. "It is no wonder that Princess Zeb wishes to include them in her bath water." Sniffing appreciatively, the eunuch exclaimed. "Oh, the fragrance! It is as close to *Jannat* as can be!"

"Well, I should have thought the marigolds are more fragrant this time of year," remarked the general dryly.

"Ah, but there is no flower as enchanting as the Mohammadi blossoms," said the eunuch, using the Persian word for roses. "And the golab that lies nestled in the heart of each bloom. It is the nectar of life! After all, did Rumi not say in one of his poems? 'The flowering season, it is over, and now the roses are dried, but the rose water retains the fragrance of the flowers.'"

"Then you should get to it right away." Jai Singh nodded grimly. "Best not to keep the Princess waiting."

He knew the flower picking was an excuse. The Princess had seen him approaching from one of her balconies and had understood that he had news. That eunuch had been sent down to ascertain what the news was.

Centuries of records had clearly determined how eunuchs with no family ties or obligations swore their complete and total loyalty to their masters or mistresses.[71] From guards to agents to servants to informers, they performed every duty with unquestioning devotion. 'All the intrigues and gossips travel through the means of this servile class.' Jai Singh recalled the words of Akbar's grand vizier, Abul Fazl, as written in his *Akbarnama* all those years back.

With a sigh, Jai Singh turned. The emperor was seated on his favourite garden diwan near the water fountain and Jai Singh covered the distance in a few long, rapid strides. No sooner was he a few steps away, than his right hand was raised toward his face, ready to offer the traditional Islamic greeting. "*Mughliya Saltnat ka iqbaal buland rahe*," he said as the emperor looked up from his task.

After his morning appearance in the Diwan-i-Aam, he had set some time aside for his favourite hobby and had been engaged for several hours. He was adept at it, his long nimble fingers moving rhythmically back and forth as he sewed. The caps were often sold to nobles in the court, and everyone appreciated the precision with which he made them.

Now as he looked at Jai Singh unsmilingly, he took a break from the sewing but did not put his needle down. The message was clear. He did not like being interrupted.

"Aali Jaan, I apologize for the intrusion. Under normal circumstances, I would never disturb you, particularly when you are in the middle of..."

"Do not beat around the bush. Come to the point, Mirza Raja."

Jai Singh shifted his head slightly in the direction of where the eunuch was standing. Far enough so as not to draw attention, yet near enough to be able to decipher the conversation, the eunuch appeared to be completely engrossed in his task of laboriously picking the freshest, most fragrant flowers for the emperor's favourite daughter.

"Aali Jaan, I understand that news has the tendency to travel like wildfire. A wise man once said, '*Deewaro ke bhi kaan hote hain*.' And the information I am now about to share is...."

"You! Come here!"

The eunuch nearly jumped out of his skin at the sound of the emperor's voice. For a minute, he didn't even realize that the emperor was talking to him. Aurangzeb had never even noticed him before.

His eyes as hard as rocks, Aurangzeb pointed a single finger at the eunuch and beckoned.

Almost tripping over his own feet, the eunuch stumbled over to where the two men waited. Bowing, he lowered his eyes and murmured. 'Aali Jaan. I am sorry. If I have done anything to annoy you, please forgive me.'

"You ask if you have done anything to annoy me. Yet you dare to stand there and ruin my morning by picking the very roses that give me pleasure."

"*Gustakhi maaf*, Aali Jaan. But...."

"And you dare to talk back! You! A lowly servant! A befitting punishment must be meted out to you."

Petrified, the eunuch turned a pleading glance at Jai Singh. With a calm smile, the general bowed to the emperor and spoke.

"Aali Jaan, please forgive him this time. I think it was the Princess who wished him to pick the flowers for her. We all know how much Princess Zeb loves roses, do we not?"

Aurangzeb stared at the eunuch with stony eyes for a few moments. Then, in a tenor that matched the expression on his face, he said, "Fifty lashes."

Beads of perspiration instantly appeared on the eunuch's forehead. His cousin had been a guard in the women's palace during Shah Jahan's reign. A minor misdemeanour had once cost him fifteen lashes, and the pain had kept him awake for weeks thereafter. Fifty lashes! He would surely die.

"Yes, fifty lashes," repeated the emperor. "That would have been a befitting punishment for someone as ignorant as you. However, since it is Princess Zeb's orders that you were following, I will let you off with a warning this time. Make sure I do not ever see you loitering about in this way again."

Nearly crying out in relief, the eunuch bowed. Apologizing profusely once again, he then scurried off in the direction of the women's palace.

"Enough time has been wasted, Mirza Raja. Let us get on. You had news."

"The news I bring is unfortunately not good, Aali Jaan. It is about the baraat that was sent to Kishengarh."

"What is it? Did a herd of wild camels attack them on their way there?"

He remained as poker faced as ever and Jai Singh could not comprehend whether he was serious or being sarcastic. Well, he was most certainly not joking. Aurangzeb rarely ever joked.

Shaking his head, Jai Singh clarified. "No, everything went smoothly in Kishengarh. The baraat received a royal welcome and, after much celebration, they departed from Kishengarh on time. It was on the way back that something completely unforeseen occurred."

"An ambush?"

Jai Singh stared in surprise. "How did you know, Aali Jaan?"

Aurangzeb shrugged. "You used the word 'unforeseen'. Well, that is what an ambush usually is. Who were they? Dacoits?"

"No, Aali Jaan. Our men were returning from Kishengarh with the Princess when they were ambushed on the way by Rana Raj Singh's forces."

"Rana Raj Singh?" A flicker of surprise passed the emperor's face on hearing the name. "I did not know he had any stake in this. If I am correct, Kishengarh and Mewar have not been on the best of terms recently. Besides, I do not suppose Raj Singh would see any benefit in assisting a small, inconsequential state like Kishengarh. There is nothing Man Singh can offer that would benefit the Rana. And undoubtedly not enough for him to offend Shahjahanabad."

The emperor was genuinely surprised to hear about Raj Singh's involvement. After the war with Dara, Aurangzeb and Raj Singh had entered into negotiations and the new emperor had agreed to all the demands that the Rajput ruler had put forth. He had assigned to the Rajput, four mahals with an enormous income and the *pargana* of

Idar. Aurangzeb had also agreed to accord him a status equivalent to Rana Sanga that enabled him to control a significant area of Mewar. The parganas of Bidnur and Mandalgarh were also assigned to him in jagir.[72] Mandalgarh had been under Kishengarh at the time. Conceding to Mewar did not go down well with the state and that was one of the major reasons for the animosity between Kishengarh and Mewar. It therefore did not make any logical sense.

"It does not make sense." Frowning, the emperor voiced his thoughts.

Jai Singh sighed. "You are right, Aali Jaan. Practically, it does not add up. But this might not be a purely practical matter. I am sure you have heard that famous tale of love by the poet Nizami Ganjavi called *Khosrow va Shirin*. The Sasanian King Khosrow Parviz II, the King of Persia, falls in love with the Armenian Princess Shirin. Farhad, who is also in love with Shirin, cuts a channel through the enormous rocks of the mighty Bisotun Mountain just so that milk can be transported to Shirin's palace. Then...."

"I find it rather astonishing that despite knowing me for as long as you have Mirza Raja, you have not yet realized how much I detest long drawn tales. Almost as much as I detest people who engage in them."

The general exhaled. "I apologize. I just wanted to state that love is an emotion that can drive people to do things that may not always make practical sense. And this is a matter of love and honour. Well, there never was a bigger motivation for a Rajput like Raj Singh."

The emperor lowered the needle and thread and placed them on the side. Leaning back into the cushions on the ample diwan, he gestured to Jai Singh to sit. It was evident that the matter was pertinent enough for him to momentarily abandon his task. The general chose one of the smaller diwans, directly facing the emperor.

"I take it that Rana Raj Singh is in love with the Princess. Hence, he has chosen to obstruct our plans."

"It certainly seems that way." Jai Singh nodded.

Aurangzeb stroked his chin thoughtfully. "So, our baraat has returned empty-handed."

Jai Singh lowered his eyes. "Yes. Though not much of the baraat remained to return."

The emperor nodded grimly. The force he'd sent to Kishengarh had been an able one. To be able to ambush such a force, to annihilate it and wipe it out, well, Rana Raj Singh was one of the rare ones who could achieve a feat like that.

Growing up, there was much that he'd heard about his great grandfather Akbar, and Rana Raj Singh's great-great-grandfather Maharana Pratap. They had been the fiercest adversaries for each other, and despite being able to establish control over most Rajput states, Akbar had been unable to do the same with Mewar. The Maharana had consistently rejected Akbar's offerings and on the contrary, had put up a mighty fight against the Mughal rule all his life. So much so that some of Akbar's closest aides had even said that the valiant Rajput often appeared in the emperor's dreams, making it difficult for him to get a good night's rest. Despite that, Akbar had held Pratap in high regard and perhaps had even had a fondness for him. There were many ministers in Akbar's court who'd even claimed that they had actually witnessed the emperor break down and weep when the news about Pratap's death had come.[73] Respect, admiration, conflict, affection, warmth. What a strange relationship it had been.

'Respect and admiration I can understand,' thought the emperor to himself then. 'But fondness and warmth! Unquestionably, those are the emotions that weaken the greatest of men. They are like the *shaitan* himself; they drive you away from ambition, they break your resolve. There is no place in my heart for passions such as these.'

"We certainly have an interesting history, the Rana and me," Aurangzeb broke the silence. "Dissent and rebellion run in his blood.

I have not forgotten how he stood by his stand during my war with my dear brother. He is tenacious, to say the least. And I can understand his affection for Charumati. She is an immeasurably beautiful woman. It would be difficult for a man to resist her charms."

There was a thoughtful look on his face, as though he was trying to work something out. Jai Singh waited patiently. He knew better than to disrupt the emperor's thought process.

The Rajputs were experts at guerilla warfare, always had been. They had proved their mettle in that area once again. The Rana had whisked the Princess away from under their noses! This ambush could most certainly break the morale of the people of Shahjahanabad. That was something that he could not allow under any circumstances.

Turning to the general, Aurangzeb ordered, "Send a messenger immediately. The fastest you can find."

"To Kishengarh, Aali Jaan?" Jai Singh looked at the emperor quizzically.

"And what use would I have with those fools?" Aurangzeb scoffed. "This matter is out of Man Singh's hands now. I do not need an oracle to tell me that Charumati herself must have written to Raj Singh and sought his help. Her poor brother had no role to play. Send a messenger to Udaipur. With a peace offering."

"A peace offering?"

The baraat had returned empty handed. Their soldiers had been killed. Would the emperor not avenge this?

"One step at a time, Mirza Raja. Haste is never a good idea. Send the peace offering. Inshallah, this matter will be resolved soon. *Takhliya*."

Jai Singh rose from the diwan. With a bow, he thanked the emperor for his time. "Shukriya, Aali Jaan. I will do the needful."

"Of course you will. As you always do."

Picking up his needle and thread, the emperor resumed his sewing. Within seconds, he was absorbed in his task once more, but a flurry of thoughts ran through the general's mind as he walked down the path. The sound of his boots broke through the calm of the otherwise silent garden.

Losing the ambush had been humiliating enough. Now this peace offering? Would that not be an indication of conceding to Mewar? Would it not demoralize the people of Shahjahanabad? Was the emperor planning something bigger? Was the peace offering a red herring? Of course, there was nothing he could do about it. His job was to follow the orders of the emperor, and that was what he intended to do.

Jai Singh walked out of the garden enclosure, past the corridors with their enormous pillars and columns, through the main entrance and then down the path that led to the narrow lanes of Meena Bazaar, the weekly market also known as *Bazaar-i-Musaqqaf*,[74] organized and enjoyed by the ladies of the royal household. Now the streets of the bazaar were empty, and the only sign of life was a flock of pigeons who had congregated in the centre, looking for seeds and other food. The roofs supported on a series of perfectly symmetrical broad arches had been designed to let in sunlight and ventilation when the ladies shopped there. Today, the morning had been bright, but sometime over the course of the past hour, the sky had turned grey and now the streets of the bazaar looked dull and dingy.

"As though in sync with my general mood," murmured Jai Singh to himself. So engrossed was he in his own thoughts that he noticed nothing else, not the pigeons, not the first call of the *maulvi* as he summoned people to the afternoon prayer or *duhr*, and not even the veiled lady who still stood on her private balcony, looking, watching, her eyes following the general as he strode through the main gates and into the labyrinth of the bazaar.

Now she had a worried expression on her face as she finally sighed and walked into her bedroom. She had seen the eunuch being reprimanded by the emperor and it was a blessing that he hadn't blurted everything out. That even though it had been Zeb-un-Nissa who had sent the eunuch to pluck the flowers, it was she, Jodhpuri Begum, who had instructed him to unearth every bit of information that he could. Bribing that eunuch had been hard, but now she wondered whether the risk had been worth it at all. He had returned empty-handed, with not even an inkling of what had transpired between the emperor and his general.

The emperor had looked composed and calm during his conversation with the general, but the quiet he was displaying could well be an ominous warning. Just like the quiet that comes before the winds change, before streaks of lightning set the sky on fire, before the thunder comes crashing down, destroying, ending everything in its way.

Jodhpuri bit her lip in frustration. Somehow, someway, she had to send a warning to Udaipur. And for that she would have to find out what the emperor's next steps were going to be. She simply had to.

CHAPTER 16

The sun hadn't risen over Udaipur yet, but through the sheer drapes at the windows, Charumati could see some light. Somewhere in the distance, a couple of roosters were heard as they got ready to welcome the break of a new day. Charumati stretched and threw off the dohar with a smile. She'd had a restful night after a long time.

"Not surprising though," she murmured to herself as she sat up in the intricately carved *sheesham* bed. "After all, there is something so reassuring, so capable, so dependable about the Rana. Now I just pray and hope that Bhai sa is also able to understand the conflict I have been going through. It breaks my heart to see how much we have grown apart in a matter of days!"

Trying to push the thoughts away, Charumati stepped down from the bed. It had been several days since her arrival in Udaipur, but the opulence of the Raj Mahal, its zenana and even this bedroom still didn't cease to amaze her. The richness of the silks, the gold and silver threadwork, the gleam of the silver, the glistening mirrors, the paintings commissioned and patronized by generations of Maharanas over the centuries. It seemed to her as though every object, every artefact, every picture, had a story of its own to tell. As though every corner of this magnificent mahal held at its core, a tale of valour, romance and sacrifice.

Charumati slipped her feet into *mojaris* and walked to the window. The sun had started its ascent by then and the first sunbeams were dancing joyfully on the surface of the water. From where she stood, Lake Pichola looked like a sparkling diamond, nestled between a string of verdant, emerald green hills. The lake had been founded by a *banjara* in the early 1300s who had diverted the water from a tributary of Kotra river by building a dam. This helped him move his animals across and transport his grains with ease. Later, Maharana Udai Singh decided to build the city of Udaipur around the lake and now it was quite literally known as 'the heart of the city'. And it certainly had Charumati's heart. There was something enigmatic about it, something that called to her, drew her to it.

"Over the years, many palaces, family mansions and temples have been built around the lake," the Rana had said to her when they had arrived in Udaipur. "Do you see that three-storied palace with the domes? That is the famed Jag Mandir built by the Sisodia family. My family."

There was a palpable tenor of pride in his voice. "It was our family's summer resort and also an asylum for those seeking refuge. Aurangzeb's father, in fact, was given refuge here before he became emperor.[75] That was the time he had revolted against his own father. He stayed here for two years. Later he took inspiration from the architecture of this great structure when he built the Taj Mahal for his wife. Their love story could melt the harshest of hearts. Strange that their son is so estranged from the emotion, is it not?"

Charumati had visibly winced at the mention of the emperor and the Rana had then changed the subject.

"You will enjoy the sunrise and sunset over the lake. Both are equally mesmerizing in different ways and the views are magnificent from every corner of the Raj Mahal."

With a shy smile, Charumati had remarked, "How nice it is to see that a brave and fearless warrior like you can be so romantic too."

"Why? Does a warrior not have a heart?"

He had laughed then, the deep throaty sound sending a shiver of nerves down her spine. She didn't know about him, but she had found it difficult to restrain her emotions ever since he'd rescued her and brought her here. Everything about him was so attractive! The dark intense eyes, strong broad shoulders, the slight curl of his moustache when he smiled. And those hands. For a warrior, they were surprisingly elegant.

When he'd offered her the right one to lead her into the palace, she'd gladly accepted. They'd walked in together, her ghoonghat concealing most of her face. She could see everything clearly though, and just like the hundreds of diyas that had illuminated the palace on that evening, her eyes had sparkled with joy at the grand welcome that had been laid out for their arrival. One of the senior members of the royal household, perhaps an aunt or older sister, had done the customary aarti even as the other women stood in the back and sang traditional folk songs. Then they were ushered into the palace amidst what seemed to be an endless shower of rose petals. Finally, the lady who had performed the aarti had summoned two daasis to show Charumati to the royal chamber that had been readied for her. In the immense relief of being rescued and then the excitement of entering the Raj Mahal, Charumati had completely forgotten her exhaustion, but it seemed to have caught up with her and she had readily followed the daasis to the zenana.

Her chamber was the last one in the corridor, with tall gilded doors that opened inwards. Laid out with expensive silks, velvety marble, plush rugs, sheesham furniture and polished silver, it was the most beautiful room Charumati had ever seen and her eyes grew wide when she walked in.

"It was Kunwar sa's instructions to get this particular room prepared for you, Rajkumari sa," remarked one of the daasis. "Other than being the loveliest chamber in the zenana, it also has the best view of the city and the lake."

The vista from the window was certainly spectacular. Strangely though, even as she stood there looking around at all the opulence and beauty, she couldn't help thinking about the home she'd left behind. The palace in Kishengarh, the courtyards, the verandahs and gardens, where she and her friends had spent hours laughing, talking, dancing. She missed it all! She missed Nirmal, too. And Bhai sa. Despite the difficult choices they'd had to make, she still loved her brother as much as before.

Later she'd taken a warm bath, eaten a meal and gone to bed. After the days she'd spent traveling in the palanquin, her body was exhausted. Her mind too was spent from all the intense worrying she'd done ever since the marriage proposal had come from Shahjahanabad. Shahjahanabad. Hazy images of the Mughal capital appeared in her dreams, making her toss and turn and murmur indiscernible things that no one could understand. She'd never been there, but she'd seen it in countless paintings, enough to evoke images that wouldn't allow her to rest. Then she'd awakened, drenched in sweat, heart beating, hands shaking. The daasis had come running and one had bathed her head with cold towels, while the other stroked her hand and made her sip a comforting concoction of turmeric and lemon juice in warm water.

"It will calm the nerves," they told her. And while it did momentarily soothe her, nothing could drive away the constant, niggling feeling of anxiety. She knew something was going to happen. The emperor would not sit quietly.

Then, as though perfectly on cue, a messenger from the Mughal court had arrived. The news had reached her almost instantly, and she'd stood on her balcony and watched with a thumping heart even as he was escorted to the durbar to deliver the message to the Rana. What was it? A threat? A warning? Or an outright declaration of war?

A peace offering from the emperor himself! That was what it turned out to be instead. She could hardly believe her ears when the daasi brought the news to her. Even as she listened with bated breath, Charumati waited for the relief to wash over her. The feeling of knowing that it was all over at last. And that she would now be safe, here in Udaipur with the Rana.

Instead of relief, however, all she felt was a growing sense of inexplicable unease. Later when she pondered over it, she wasn't surprised at her trepidation. She'd smashed the emperor's painting under the sole of her foot. She'd cursed him and his empire. The Rana had ambushed and destroyed the baraat he had sent. In which irrational world did someone like Aurangzeb forgive such actions and propose peace?

The thought had gnawed at her for hours, taking over her senses, consuming her so completely that she'd been unable to sleep at all that night. And it had been the same the following night. The third night had been a little better, but only because she'd given in to exhaustion and dropped off as soon as her head touched the pillow. She had awakened in the middle of the night, though, and once again the daasis had come.

The news had then reached the Rana. Princess Charumati was distraught, and nobody could calm her down. "She is obviously frightened about the ordeal she has been through and worried about what is to come," said the Rana's aunt to him. "Not to mention the heartbreak she is going through on account of her brother. It is like a betrayal of blood."

"Man Singh has not had it easy since the day he ascended the throne. What with the manner in which his father died and the fact that he was such a young boy himself, the circumstances of his accession were hardly ideal." Raj Singh shrugged. "Though that does not justify his decision with regard to his sister; certainly, does not befit a Rajput."

"Well, right now, my concern is for Charumati. She has been very brave, but now she needs someone to reassure her that she is indeed safe here."

Raj Singh knew that he was the only one who could offer that assurance. He went to see Charumati the same evening. She was in her sitting room, admiring the paintings from her vantage point on the couch. It was a beautiful couch, its back inlaid with delicate mirror work and floral mosaics in turquoise and emerald green.

"You look like a painting yourself," smiled the Rana as he approached her and she started to rise. "No, no, please do not get up. I will join you."

He settled down in the armchair opposite the couch. "You like the paintings?" he asked her, glancing at the wall. They were an assortment of scenes from Rajput courts and hunting expeditions.

"They are certainly spectacular works of art." Charumati nodded. "I understand that Udaipur was one of the first centres of art that was established along with Bikaner, Jodhpur, Amber and Bundi."

"Yes, many decades ago," agreed the Rana. "Though of course the subjects back then were essentially inspired by the Bhakti movement and based on book illustrations from texts like the Ramayana."[76]

"I find it rather strange," said Charumati with a wry smile. "That even though the goddesses were depicted often enough in those paintings, there is now an absence of works that feature women. I cannot but be chagrined at this distinction, though I know that most of the women from the royal household are usually not in the public eye. Hence the difference."[77]

"You are a perceptive woman." The Rana looked impressed. "And brave too. In fact, braver and bolder than most men. I was, therefore, rather astonished when I heard that you have been panicking."

There was a short silence. Charumati suddenly felt completely tongue-tied.

"As you pointed out yourself, Mewar has always been a centre of art and my family has patronized some of the greatest painters over the decades," continued the Rana. "I, too, enjoy discussing art and other forms of creative expression. However, right now, I think there are other more pressing matters that need attention. You have been unable to rest or sleep ever since you came here. May I ask why?"

Even as she lowered her eyes, Charumati could feel the Rana's gaze on her.

When she finally looked up, the anxiety that she had been harbouring for so long was palpably visible on her face. "I worry Rana ji," she cried out then. "I worry all the time! I feel a sense of dread, a foreboding. As though a cold hand is wrapped around my heart and is constantly squeezing it, not letting me breathe. I cannot...."

"Do you not trust me?"

His words silenced her instantly, and she looked at him in embarrassment. "Of course I trust you. How can I not? That is why I wrote to you. I knew that you were the only one who could help me. But Rana ji, that emperor! He is not to be trusted."

"I was talking about trusting me, not trusting him."

"Yes, but that letter, that peace offering! Something about it just does not ring true."

"There was a painting along with the letter you had sent through that messenger. A resplendently beautiful painting of Lord Krishna and Rukmani. Am I correct?"

Charumati nodded, her brows furrowed in confusion at the sudden change in the subject.

"Yes," she answered his question. "I sent the painting for you. I trust the messenger handed it over to you and it is now safely in your possession?"

Pulling his chair forward, the Rana leaned in closer. Now they were only inches apart from each other.

"I did not accept the painting from your messenger. I will tell you why. After Lord Krishna rescued Rukmani, he brought her back to Dwarka, where he married her. She had placed her trust in him, as you have placed yours in me. It is my duty to protect and honour the woman I love. I will therefore only accept the painting after I have done my duty as well, and made you my queen."

It was the first time he had admitted his love for her. Blushing, the Princess raised her head and looked at him. Their eyes locked and instantly, everything else around them dissipated. The myriad hues of the paintings they had admired just a few moments ago seemed to scatter away like a rainbow does when the sun comes out. Even the sounds around them, the gentle trickling of water from the marble fountain in the centre of the room, the meowing of peacocks on the terrace outside, everything grew softer, muffled, as though fading away into the distance, giving in to a silence that seemed strangely monumental. It was as if now there was no more need for words, as if now they could comprehend the unspoken between them. For that brief period, Charumati felt as though she was in a trance, a reverie that she didn't want to awaken from. His dark eyes bore into hers, as though he was trying to convey something, a promise, a commitment that he would give up everything to honour her, to protect her. And just like that, every fear, every misgiving disappeared and in place arose a confidence, an assurance that she now had nothing to worry about. This was now her home, and she would be safe here.

"Oh, I almost forgot to tell you." The Rana smiled, breaking the spell. "There is a kite flying game happening in the city this evening. The skyline will be alive like nothing you have seen before. I think you will enjoy it very much."

Charumati smiled back at him. "I will certainly participate. I happen to believe that the tradition of kite flying represents the soaring spirit. There is an unbound joy about it."

"The soaring spirit! That is indeed a wonderful description of this ancient tradition that has been practiced by our ancestors since time immemorial."

They chatted for a few more minutes and then a daasi knocked softly on the door. She had brought with her a silver bowl, and she set it down on the side table. Then with folded hands, she bowed to the Rana.

"*Ghanni khamma*, Hukum."

Turning to the Princess, she bowed once again. "Ghanni khamma, Rajkumari sa."

"Khamma Ghani." Charumati glanced at the silver bowl. "What is in it?" she asked with interest.

"It is a paste of rosewater and honey," said the daasi. "The long journey and lack of sleep have taken a toll on you. This paste will restore your natural glow. It used to be Rani Padmini's favourite regimen every morning."

"Well, I will leave you to it then." The Rana rose from his chair.

Five minutes later, he was sitting down at the sprawling sheesham desk in his study. Putting the quill to paper, he started writing. It was a short letter and barely took him a few minutes to complete. That was not surprising since Rana Raj Singh was a focused man and hardly ever hesitated once he had taken a decision. Finishing the letter, he slipped it into an envelope which he promptly sealed and then turned over to address.

Ratan Singh Chundawat, Jodh Niwas, Salumbar, Mewar.

Who else would he turn to at a time like this? After all, the two families went back a long way. The Chundawats were the descendants of Chunda Sisodia, the fifteenth century Mewari prince and the eldest son of Rana Lakha. After surrendering his right to the throne of Mewar, Chunda Sisodia had acquired the supreme position of advisor to the reigning Rana on all political and military matters and an unparalleled status in the royal council. His descendants came to be known as the Chundawat clan and for centuries, the two families had fought side by side on the battlefield.

"Oh Ratan!" sighed the Rana. "It pains me to ask you for help, particularly at a time like this, but I have no option."

The chieftain had recently been married to Sahal Kanwar, also known as Hadi Rani, the daughter of Hada Chauhan Rajput. It had not even been a week since the nuptials and Raj Singh felt very guilty involving him in this battle. He did, however, know that his friend would never let him down. Beyond everything, this was a matter of principles and pride.

The Rana picked up the sealed envelope and strode out of his study. Outside, preparations for the upcoming kite flying game were already in full swing as people started congregating on the terraces. "Will you be joining us later, Bhai sa?" asked one of the Rana's younger cousins, showing him the kite he meant to use for the game.

"Not today. But you have a good time with your friends and cousins." With a quick smile, the Rana hurried on. He might have tempted Charumati to join the game, but kite flying was the furthest thing from his own mind. Thankfully, the distance to Salumbar was only seventy kilometres and the letter would most definitely reach Ratan Singh Chundawat in time. In the meantime, the Rana had a plan to make.

He might have appeared blasé in front of the Princess, but the truth was that this was not the time to be nonchalant. The message that had arrived from Delhi yesterday had kept him awake the entire night. Jodhpuri Begum hadn't been privy to the conversation that had happened between Aurangzeb and his general Jai Singh. She had, however, known enough to send him a concerned and timely warning.

Do not take the peace offering at face value. There is more to it. Please be prepared.

The message had been brief, even the handwriting was evident of the fact that it had been written by someone in a tearing hurry. The Rana had read it several times to make sure that he didn't miss anything. Then, knowing how perilous it could be for the begum if anyone found it, he had torn the paper into minuscule pieces, but not before inwardly thanking the begum. After writing to Charumati about seeking his support, this was the second time she had come to their help. How brave and fearless she was! But that wasn't surprising, was it? After all, she was a *Rajputain.*

Chapter 17

The celebratory air in Salumbar's Jodh Niwas Palace hadn't yet abated. It had been several days since the bride had entered her new home, but the post marriage ceremonies were still on in full swing. The palace's domed *gumbads,* circular terraces, archways and pillars were polished and decorated with fresh flowers every morning. New diyas were lit at sundown, the shimmering wicks softly reflected on the floral frescoed ceilings. Even the murals that adorned the walls and columns now seemed to come alive and blush in anticipation of this wonderful new phase that lay ahead for the Chundawat chieftain and his bride.

After the traditional welcome aarti, the most important ritual was the *mooh dikhai.* According to custom, this introduction of the bride to the groom's family was held with much pomp and fanfare. The new bride received gifts and jewellery in abundance from friends and relatives, including special heirloom jewels which had been in the Chundawat family for decades. Of course, the ceremonies did not end there. In fact, in the days that followed, hundreds of people continued to pour into the palace to offer their congratulations to the couple and accept the generous hospitality that the Chundawats were famous for. Copious quantities of ghee were dumped into enormous *kadhais* and the delicious fragrance of frying *kachoris* and sweetmeats made sure that nobody left the palace without eating their fill. Sounds of music and dance filled the courtyards day and night, and even the older members of the zenana joined the traditional ghoomar to commemorate the joyous occasion.

"Panna Baisa! *Sambhal ke!*" One of Ratan's aunts laughed when she saw her older sister join the circle of dancing women one evening. "Your ghoomar days are over unless you want a stitch in your waist."

This was followed by a lot of jovial laughing. The older lady waved her sister's suggestion away and continued pirouetting with the others. The dholak got louder and the twinkling diyas gave way to majestic *mashaals*, the entire palace illuminated by their blazing torches.

And in the midst of all the celebration, among the hundreds of people who came and went over that week, the groom and the bride noticed no one but each other. Ratan Singh's eyes were constantly on Sahal's luminous face as she sat across him in a crowded room, smiling as they played the traditional wedding games. He let her win each one, and she looked away bashfully when the other women teased him for having lost his heart to her already. "A strapping warrior chieftain like you!" remarked one of Ratan Singh's sisters. "We never imagined that you would get besotted."

"But we cannot blame Bhaisa, can we?" a cousin laughed gleefully. "Bhabhisa is so beautiful, it would be difficult not to be smitten."

Ratan Singh tried to keep a poker face after that, but it was difficult to conceal the love and ardent admiration he felt for Sahal. Her beauty was one thing, but the grace and elegance she possessed drew him to her like a magnet. And the quiet strength behind that smile. As though she could carry the weight of the world on those delicate shoulders. One look at her and you were sure that here was a woman who would not be deterred or daunted by anything. A true

Rajputain. He tried to imagine what it would be like if everyone else present in the room suddenly vanished and only the two of them were left. How he longed to be alone with her now. There was so much to say to each other, so much to discover.

Even as he looked at her, her eyes seemed to speak directly to him. *We have our whole lives in front of us, Raja sa. Many, many wonderful years to know, love and cherish each other. Soon this crowd will disappear, and the voices will hush. Then the only voice that I will hear will be yours, and you will hear mine.*

They exchanged a surreptitious smile across the room, their hearts beating in anticipation as the games and festivities continued well into the wee hours of the morning. And the next day. And the next. Until it was time for the wedding guests and extended family to leave. They bestowed the newlywed couple with the choicest of blessings, for a long and joyous married life, a very prosperous and happy kingdom and, of course, a wonderful son to inherit the title.

And then finally, it was just them. Corner to corner, the enormous room was adorned with strings of fragrant marigolds, roses and *raat ki raani*. Sahal, dressed in a blushing red ghagra, choli and odhni waited for her husband by the window. Outside, the full moon gleamed and the silence of the night was punctuated only by the call of the nightjars, those grey-brown nocturnal birds native to the arid climate of the desert. Their shrill voices sounded like whistles as they called to each other from one end of the terrace to the other, and it almost sounded to Sahal as though they were having a conversation.

"In a language known only to them," she said aloud to herself with fascination.

"Yes, just like us."

He'd been so quiet, she hadn't heard him enter. Now he smiled when she turned around, and they walked toward each other. A glass of milk simmered for hours and seasoned with ground cardamom and saffron had been placed on the side table and Sahal picked it up and proffered it to Ratan Singh. Accepting it, he bade her to join him on the diwan. "Come Sahal. I have waited many days for this moment. There is so much I want to say to you, so much I want to hear."

"You echo my thoughts, Raja sa."

They sat down together on the diwan, and he gathered her in his arms. Minutes passed, then hours, but the fragrance of the flowers did not wane. The moon climbed higher in the sky, bathing the room in its silver light. Even as it cast its glow upon Sahal's face, Ratan Singh thought that he had never before seen a more beautiful woman in his life. She was radiant, ethereal, and he found himself falling more deeply in love with her than he had ever thought possible. And he knew that she felt the same way about him. That she too felt drawn to him in a way that was otherworldly, a connection that seemed to transcend even time. Sleep was the last thing on their minds that night and as they loved and laughed and talked, secrets were revealed and souls were bared.

She awoke and bathed early the next morning, in time for the Gauri pooja that had to be performed by the bride before sunrise. Ratan Singh was sleeping peacefully, and she smiled as she stood at the bedside, looking at him. It was dark in the room and his face looked tranquil in sleep, the features gently silhouetted against the soft light. Draping the heavy odhni around her head, Sahal tiptoed out of the room. The pooja was being held in the palace temple located within the periphery. Sahal, who was a keen observer of directions, started walking toward it with the familiar, confident steps of a woman who knew her way around. So much so that to many, it might have been difficult to believe that it had merely been a week since she had arrived in Salumbar.

Her husband was still asleep when she returned an hour later. She crept in as quietly as she'd left and was just about to close the heavy brass door when she heard frantic footsteps outside. "Rani sa, Rani sa!" It was mere a whisper but there was an urgency to the voice that made Sahal rush to the doorstep at once. A daasi stood there, waiting with an anxious look on her face.

"What is it?" Sahal inquired. "Why have you come here at this time? I have only just returned from the Gauri Pooja."

"Rani sa, please forgive me for the intrusion. There is an urgent message for Hukum, which has to be delivered to him immediately."

"An urgent message? From where?"

"Udaipur, Rani sa. Rana Raj Singh has personally sent a messenger with the letter."

"Rana Raj Singh!" Sahal didn't need to be apprised of the relationship that Salumbar shared with Udaipur. She was well aware of the fact that if the Rana had sent a message for Ratan Singh, it had to be delivered without a moment's delay. "Ask Vikram Singh to bring the letter to us right away." Sahal knew the letter's contents had to be confidential and Vikram Singh was one of Ratan Singh's most trusted men. "Hurry now!"

The daasi turned and ran down the path. Then Sahal went inside to awaken her husband, gently closing the door behind her.

Minutes later, they sat side-by-side on the bed, still unmade from the previous night. The letter from Udaipur had been read several times and now lay face down between them. Outside, the sky had turned pink, but there was still some time remaining for sunrise. Picking up the silver *lota* from the bedside table, Sahal poured water into a tumbler and handed it to Ratan Singh. He took a few sips and then placed the glass back on the table.

"When Rana Sanga fought Babur in the Battle of Khanwa, my clansmen were there by the Rana's side." Ratan Singh looked at his wife. "Then, when Maharana Pratap went to war, it was my family that supported him and braved Akbar's formidable forces in the Battle of Haldighati. Our clan has been fighting alongside Udaipur for generations. As for Raj Singh, he is like a brother, a dear friend to me."

"I did wonder why he could not attend our wedding." Sahal smiled wistfully. "Now we know."

"Yes, I had received a letter from him, apologizing for his absence. Of course, he did not mention then what his reasons were."

Sahal fiddled with the bangles on her left lower arm. There were nine of them, the white ivory dyed a deep blushing red. "Do you know what *Mami sa* told me about these bangles just before the vidaai?" There was a pensive look in her kohled eyes.

Ratan Singh stared at his wife in surprise. He was confused at the sudden change in the subject.

"What? That they look resplendent on your lovely arms? My dear, this might not be such a good time for vanity." He smiled at her indulgently. She looked so beautiful, her flawless skin glowing in the early morning light, the long dark hair still damp from her bath. It was difficult to even imagine leaving her and going away.

"No, my dear." Sahal shook her head. "Mami sa told me that these bangles are never to be removed because they are so much more than mere adornments. These bangles are representative of a happy marriage. They are symbolic of the husband's health and happiness. And his long life."[78]

Ratan Singh pulled Sahal close to him and she rested her head on his shoulder. The couple looked out of the open window as the sun began its ascent over the crescent-shaped dunes in the distance. "It is going to be a hot day," remarked Ratan Singh. "The sun has a fiercely determined look about it this morning."

"As do you." Sahal nodded. "After all, you are a Suryavanshi[79] Rajput. I know what your heart is telling you. Please listen to it."

"How can I? My heart does not belong to me anymore."

"Do not feel torn. I know you love me. But right now, your duty is elsewhere."

A sudden gust of wind lifted the letter from the bed, making it fly across the room. It landed with a flutter on the marble floor. Sahal rose from the bed. Picking up the letter, she handed it to her husband.

"This clearly states that their need is urgent. There is no time for procrastination or hesitation. You must leave for Udaipur immediately."

"But Sahal, my love, not even a week has gone by and..."

"We have many, many years of happiness ahead of us. Why then worry about a week? Our life together will begin after you return. Until then, I will wait for you here."

Ratan Singh took Sahal's hands in his own and pressed them gently. "I want to be fair to you, Sahal," he said. "Just looking at you now, so beautiful and trusting, I cannot bear to do this."

"You are a warrior first." Sahal pulled her hands away and walked toward the dressing area of the room. When she returned a minute later, she was carrying Ratan Singh's talwar in both her hands. The reverence and awe with which she carried the weapon was palpable to her husband.

"This," she continued, holding the sword out to Ratan, "Is your first and foremost duty. The talwar that represents the Goddess herself. Surely, you will never forget the *Karga Shapna*. Your rite of passage which allows you to use this talwar in order to protect those who need your help. In this case, it is a woman. There is no question about it. You have to do your duty."

Ratan Singh held his hands out, palms facing up. Sahal carefully placed the talwar in them. "I hear Aurangzeb's army is supposed to be a formidable force," she said. Her face was calm, her voice steady.

"Yes, that is what I have heard too," Ratan Singh nodded, his expression grim. "The ambush carried out by the Rana was successful. An open encounter in the battlefield is a completely different challenge."

"I am confident." Sahal lifted her eyes. "You will fight fairly and fearlessly because that is what your *dharma* tells you to do.[80] And with Bhavani Ma's blessing, Mewar will emerge victorious."

"With a valiant and courageous woman like you by my side, there is no more to be said. I should get my force ready and set off at once." Ratan Singh pulled Sahal into a tight embrace. "I will miss you Sahal. Please take care of yourself in my absence."

She clung to him but did not allow a single tear to fall. *Never bid your dear ones goodbye with tears,* her mother had always said. *It is not auspicious.*

Sahal took the sword from her husband's hands and smiled. "I know you will be meeting with the diwan and *senapati.* In the meantime, I will clean this sword myself. When you ride into the battle, do not forget that I am with you. Every moment, every step of the way."

He left the room an hour later. The broad back was ramrod straight, the stride determined and confident. After his meeting, would be the puja and ritualistic sacrifice without which no Rajput ever entered the battlefield. Then, he would finally wear the armour, an honour and privilege for every Rajput warrior.

As he walked out and closed the door behind him, Sahal's gaze shifted to the window on her left. It was the only east-facing window in the room and as she looked out, she saw that the sun was now high up in the sky. Carefully placing Ratan Singh's sword on the diwan, Sahal walked to the window. Offering prayers to the Surya God was a tradition among Suryavanshi Rajputs. The descendants of the sun. The centre of the universe. The source of all energy and power. Now as she folded her hands, the bangles on her arms made a tinkling sound, their crimson colour deepening under the blaze of the sun rays. With a small smile, Sahal bowed her head in reverence and completed her prayers. Then, with a renewed sense of conviction, she retrieved the sword from the diwan and went back inside to polish it.

CHAPTER 18

In Mewar, leading his force into the battle was considered one of the most important duties of the king. And with the king leading from the front, it was not surprising that every man was willing to wield a sword or muskat if the need arose. In fact, historically, every Mewari man was considered a soldier, a warrior. Intense emotion and an infallible sense of duty was one prerequisite of a strong force. The other necessity was tactical strategy and structure.

Every Mewari ruler over the years had been well aware of the importance of tactical military strategy. It would actually not be an exaggeration to say that this was one of the key factors that determined the fate of a force in the battlefield. Tactics were a critical aspect of Mewari warfare. An example would be the recruitment of *haraval* troops. These were mostly informants or spies who were sent well in advance to obtain critical information about the enemy's activities, position, and strength. While some tried and tested strategies had remained constant over the years, others had gone through fundamental changes. From understanding the supremacy of an armoured cavalry as was ascertained during the Battle of Khanwa, to adopting new weapons that enabled the infantry to defeat the cavalry in an open encounter, to specifically training the forces to be fast moving and mobile during the reign of Maharana Pratap, the Mewari forces had dominated the battlefields of Rajputana through the centuries.

Maharana Pratap, of course, was known as much for his valour and tenacity, as he was for the ease with which he adopted novel and unconventional tactics in warfare. Not only did he discover the skills of guerilla warfare in India, but he also became a master at the 'scorched earth policy' which aimed at destroying everything that was important to the enemy including assets like weapons, crops, livestock, transport vehicles, communication sites, and industrial resources. It was the amalgamation of his valiant resistance to the enemy and the astuteness he displayed in strategy that made him a force to be reckoned with. It was no wonder then that he was revered as one of the strongest warriors the subcontinent had ever seen.

Now while there was much that Raj Singh learnt from the tactics employed by Maharana Pratap, there was one thing that he naturally had in common with him. He was masterfully adept at inventing new and innovative methods to strengthen the Mewari forces. Not only had he assessed how to attack the enemy in their own territory, he was also capable of countering their vandalism with the same ferocity as was meted out by them. This was sufficiently evident from the raids he had conducted in Gujarat and Idar. Surprise and night attacks were equally common, and it was clear that under his reign, the Mewari troops were no more compelled to practice warfare with the limitations of traditional methods. Raj Singh was a practical and radical realist[81], a quality which made him, much like his ancestor, a formidable foe for the Mughals.

There was a structured hierarchy that was abided by in important campaigns and the Maharana was followed by other high-ranking officers like the Pradhan, Diwan, Senapati and Bakshi. Senior officers were usually appointed by the king himself and, when required, he could call upon his trusted noblemen who maintained regular contingents. These jagiri forces could be absorbed and used as needed, and skilled gunners and instructors were recruited with care. After the Battle of Khanwa, the army of Mewar was divided into infantry, cavalry, elephant corps, camel corps, and artillery. The infantry, also known as *paidalsena* comprised soldiers wielding swords, shields, spears, lances and matchlocks. They wore helmets and a complete armour for protection since they engaged in hand-to-hand fighting. The cavalry, though, was one of the army's strengths since Mewar was a mine of horses. Maharana Pratap had been witness to how the Mughals had, in many a campaign, managed to take the enemy by surprise because of the speed and mobility of their cavalry, and he started paying more attention to this division of Mewar's army. Mewar's horses were famed for being strong and swift and there were both Rajputs and non-Rajputs in the cavalry. The horsemen used armour, helmets and carried swords, bow and arrow, mace and battle axes as weapons. Special care was taken to ensure that the horses were also equipped with the right kind of fittings to make the horsemen as agile as possible. For instance, the saddles were designed keeping in mind that the horsemen be able to stand completely upright if needed, but that was just one example. The cavalry was the pride of Mewar's army and keen attention was paid to the training of the *ghudsawars*, as well as to the health of the horses.

Next in line were the elephant and camel corps. Historically, most Mewari rulers had led their armies on the elephant backs. The significance of this division could therefore not be undermined, and the best mahavats were recruited to train and care for the enormous beasts. There were some exceptions to this general rule, though, the most famed being Maharana Pratap and his loyal horse Chetak. And considering that Raj Singh had followed his great-great-grandfather's example in so many critical matters, it was not surprising that he too always led his army on horseback. As for the camels, they were mostly imported from Bikaner and Jodhpur and the division was headed by the *daroga*. The fact that a camel could accommodate two riders instead of one, and could carry heavy supplies across difficult terrain, made them a useful mode of transport during battle.

There were several lessons that the Mewari army had learnt over the years and investing in a robust artillery division was one of them. After Rana Sangram Singh lost to the first Mughal emperor Babur in the Battle of Khanwa, one of the reasons cited by experts and eyewitnesses was Babur's excellent artillery division. Following this defeat, Mewar made it a point to focus on building a strong artillery that was equipped with the best and latest cannons, and there had been no turning back after that. Now Mewar had an excellent artillery division, furnished with both heavy and light cannons. In the battlefield, every cannon was assigned to a gunner, and the heavy ones were pulled by bullocks, camels and even elephants.[82]

And that was how Mewar readied itself for the possibility of war. 'Though this is not just any war,' thought Raj Singh to himself one evening. 'This is about protecting the woman I love.' He had noticed that after his visit that day, Charumati had calmed down visibly. She still looked anxious sometimes. Everyone in the palace did. It would be hard not to, what with everything that was going on. But that incessant worrying, that constant apprehension, that had certainly ceased. And the report from the zenana was positive too. She no longer woke up in the middle of the night, drenched in sweat, hands shaking. It was a validation of how much she trusted him.

'I cannot let her down now that she has placed her absolute faith in me. We simply cannot leave any stone unturned.'

Raj Singh nodded grimly as he walked out onto his terrace and looked down at Lake Pichola. The calmness of its waters always soothed him and it was what he needed right now, for it had been a busy day. He had visited the *karkhana*, *darukhana* and *ambarkhana* to take stock of supplies himself that morning. Following that, he had had a long and detailed discussion with his pradhan, diwan and senapati. The meeting had been positive, and they had been quick to reassure him. They were ready, determined and raring to go. And Ratan Singh Chundawat's prompt response had boosted their morale even more. He was on his way to Udaipur with his best force. Now all they had to do was wait for the Mughals to attack. Knowing that it was inevitable, Raj Singh could only hope that it would soon be over.

***

When the Mughals came to India from Central Asia, they also brought with them a Central Asian military tradition. Prior to their arrival, battles were fought on horse and elephant back with the use of bows and arrows, shields, swords and other weapons. The Mughals brought gunpowder, and with it the use of artillery, muskets and bombs. The artillery division was in fact, responsible for the triumphant Mughal victory in the historic Battle of Panipat which led to the overthrow of the Lodi empire and the firm establishment of Mughal rule. Artillery or *topkhana* as it was called, went through rapid upgradation over the centuries and Aurangzeb too like his ancestors, had ensured that his military used the latest, most sophisticated weaponry.

The structure of the Mughal military was divided into cavalry, infantry and artillery. Elephants and horses were used in large numbers. When on the march, the heavy artillery went first, followed by units of the infantry called advance guards. The baggage came next, with the camels carrying the imperial treasure and then the royal kitchen. This was finally followed by the army. The *Mir Tuzak* or Lord of Arrangement was given the responsibility of identifying the route, taking a decision about the marches, when and how to proceed and selecting sites for laying out the encampments. While at camp, each soldier was assigned a tent of his own. Outside the main enclosure rested the elephants, horses, the carts and litters and the hunting leopards. The heavy artillery was placed at a distance to defend the approach.[83]

Now, arrangements were on at a frenetic pace in Shahjahanabad. Knowing the tenacity of the Mewaris, the Mughal forces had to ensure that they were fully equipped with sufficient weaponry as well as supplies. Unlike the Mewaris who travelled simply and could manage with a water mug, ammunition bag, basic clothes, some money and their *baphla bati*, the Mughals were used to elaborate arrangements and ample baggage. Used for royal tours and military expeditions, 'the imperial camp' as it was called, was so enormous in scale that it was often compared to a mobile, de facto capital city. Size notwithstanding, it was also factors like technology, tactics, operations, training, and logistics that made the imperial force unparalleled for its foes. Of course, one of the biggest assets of any force had to be its senior officers or generals. The Mughal army, too, had its share of those steadfastly brave and fiercely loyal officers who could give up their lives in the battlefield. And among them was a particularly valiant and fearless general, Jalal Khan Rohilla.

Jalal Khan Rohilla was a pathan from the Pashtun Daudzai tribe of Kandahar. The tribe were the descendants of Daud, the grandson of Ghoria from whom the Ghoria Khel, a Pashtun sub-tribe, had emerged. Having come from Kandahar, the Ghoria Khel then moved to Ghazni, Kabul, Ningrahar and Peshawar, and eventually gained control over the whole of Afghanistan. Jalal, though, was born in

India. His father was Nawab Darya Khan Rohilla, a horse trader from Barbar village in Afghanistan. Darya Khan later went on to serve as a mansabdar in the court of the fourth Mughal emperor, Jehangir.

Jehangir's father, Akbar, though was not known to have had a particularly favourable attitude toward the Afghans. One reason might have been his belief that the Afghans were entering the subcontinent in big numbers, as well as their tribal attitude and large landholdings. Another factor was that admission into the Mughal service was through recruitment from the family members of old nobles. It was not surprising, therefore, that very limited Afghan mansabs were found in service during Akbar's reign.

It was, in fact, Jehangir who found the Afghans to be faithful to his crown and gave them a position of authority along with generous *mansabs*. Impressed with their loyalty and commitment, he even allowed the trustworthy Afghans to bring their friends and family into India, offering them employment and a means to make a living. This trend was followed by his son Shah Jahan and by the end of his reign, many Afghanis had migrated and settled in India.[84] Among them was Jalal's family as well.

Jalal's father Nawab Darya Khan Rohilla was introduced into Jehangir's court by Khan Jahan Lodi, an Afghan who was a close aide of the emperor and had gained a position of importance in the court. This had happened over time, since Lodi's father Daulat Khan Lodi had been one of the few Afghans who had been close to Jehangir's father Akbar. After Daulat Khan's death, his son Pir Khan entered the service of Abdur Rahim Khan Khanan, a famed poet and one of the nine most important ministers of Akbar's court. Pir Khan gradually rose in rank and was summoned to the court by Jehangir soon after his succession. Pir Khan was given the rank of 3000/1500, the title of 'Salabat Khan' as well as 'Farzand' or beloved son. He was later promoted to the rank of 5000/500 and given the title of 'Khan-i-jahan'. What was surprising about his rising influence was that he had neither served in any major military or administrative campaign until that time, nor had he served Jehangir in his princehood. It was evident then that there were two major reasons why he was favoured by the emperor. One was his general manner and charm, and the second was the fact that Jehangir wanted to reassure the Afghan community by promoting one of them. Khan Jahan's ancestry made him a perfect means for such a motivation. Such was his influence that Emperor Jehangir even wanted to marry him into the royal family. This proposal was humbly refused by Pir Khan, stating that the honour only be reserved for the princes.[85]

It was ultimately Khan Jahan Lodi who took Darya Khan Rohilla under his wing, later recommending to the emperor to grant Darya a high ranking. Lodi's downfall though happened just as swiftly as his rise, taking Darya with him. Lodi, by then, had become one of Jehangir's biggest confidantes and was staunchly loyal to the emperor. When Prince Khurram fell out with Noor Jahan and rebelled against Jehangir's reign, Jehangir appointed Lodi commander-in-chief of the army. Following that, Lodi did not support Khurram as an heir, despite the fact that many of the Afghan tribes had declared their allegiance. According to the *Padshahnama*, Lodi then went through a period of psychological insecurities and in 1629, tried to escape to the court of the Nizam Shah in the Deccan. He was hunted down by Shah Jahan's forces, following which he and his entourage turned toward Punjab. They couldn't escape and Darya Khan was slain in the conflict. As for Khan Jahan, even though he did manage to get away then, he too was eventually hunted down and killed in 1631 in Sihanda in Central India.[86]

Subsequently, Darya's two sons, Bahadur Khan and Jalal Khan, also entered the Mughal service. During Aurangzeb's reign, Jalal bravely and valiantly served the Mughal army and proved his commitment to the crown. As a recognition of his valour and loyalty, he was later bestowed with the title of '*Diler Khan*' by Aurangzeb. Now he was one of the senior generals in the army, one of the very few who the emperor trusted to lead and command strategically important battles. And the battle with Udaipur was of vital importance. It was therefore not surprising that when the Mughal forces departed from Shahjahanabad toward Udaipur on that fateful day, it was general Diler Khan who had been placed in charge.

CHAPTER 19

It was a sudden shuddering that awakened her, the kind she'd never experienced before. At first, she thought it was a dream, but then her eyes snapped open and she listened intently, trying to understand. There had been a storm the previous night with howling winds that had kept her and most of the palace awake anyhow. She had finally managed to fall into a deep slumber at around three in the morning but now she sat up with a jolt, her heart hammering loudly against her chest. A quick glance at the window confirmed that it was still dark outside, and the storm had quietened. The rumbling, though, continued, a low ominous sound that seemed to be coming from afar, yet building up fast enough to make the floor beneath her shudder and shake.

"What... what is happening?" Charumati stepped down from the bed, clutching the nearest column for support. Even as she stood there, attempting to balance herself, the brass *jhoomar* on the ceiling started swaying, each one of its twenty-one bulbs quivering visibly.

"Rajkumari sa! Rajkumari sa!"

The bedroom door was flung open, and Charumati stared at the daasi in astonishment. The fact that she hadn't knocked, instead taking the liberty to throw open the door herself, meant that this was an emergency.

"What is it?"

"Rajkumari sa, it is the Mughals! The fauj has reached the outskirts of Udaipur!"

The room instantly spun around Charumati. Her knees gave way, and she stumbled to the floor, even as the daasi ran to help her. Pouring water from the pitcher on the bedside table, she helped the Princess back to the bed. Then she made her take several sips from the copper glass.

It took many seconds, but the water seemed to revive the Princess. Turning to the daasi, she said, "The shuddering must have been the horses' hooves."

"Ji sa. The horses, elephants, cannons. It is an enormous army, almost as though the city of Shahjahanabad itself has arrived here. At least that is what I heard."

"And Rana ji? Where is he?" She was trying hard not to panic.

"I am right here."

Both women turned, the daasi simultaneously reaching for her odhni. Drawing her ghoonghat, she bowed her head. The Rana's imposing frame filled the doorway, though in the silhouetted shadows it was difficult to make out the expression on his face.

"Thank you for your help, Ganga. I will now request you to leave, since I want to speak to the Princess alone. Ekaant!" The Rana spoke calmly, though the voice had the usual tenor of authority that made it so distinctive. This time, though, Charumati noticed something different about his tone. There was an urgency, a sense of criticality which made two things instantly clear. The graveness of the situation and the paucity of time.

"Ji Hukum!" The daasi was on her feet and out of the room within seconds. No sooner had she disappeared down the long, checkered corridor than Raj Singh shut the door behind him. Even as he approached the Princess, she noticed the gleaming talwar in his hand. However, it was only when he was a couple of feet away that she realized that he had already changed into the pristine white cloth with the red waistband that was a sure sign of the fact that Mewar was now officially going to war. Wound tightly about the waist and pulled between the legs, this was the clothing that the Rajput kings wore just before they performed the customary pre-war pooja and *pashubali*.

"I have entrusted you with the impossible, have I not?" Charumati looked into the eyes of the man she loved, the man who was now staking everything for the sake of her honour, her life. "Today, because of me, Mewar is going to war."

"No, my dear." Raj Singh smiled. "Mewar has been at war for many, many decades. Mewar has never given up the fight, has never succumbed, never submitted. You know that as well as I do."

The lump in her throat didn't allow her to speak, even as she forced the unshed tears back. Trying to quell the tremor she felt in her legs, Charumati walked to her dressing table and picked up the tiny silver *dani*, filled to the brim with sindoor. Without wasting a single second, she brought it back to Raj Singh. Dipping the third finger of her right hand in the dani, she then smeared his forehead with a deep crimson *tilak*, the sacred mark that was believed to be an assurance of victory.

The Rana then proffered his sword to her. Charumati, of course, didn't need to be told. She knew exactly what she had to do. For a Rajput, his sword was no less than a deity and *shastra puja* was a common practice. Dipping her finger once again into the dani, the Princess now smeared the glistening talwar with the same sindoor.

The Rana smiled. "You will be happy to know that my dear friend Ratan Singh arrived last night with his force."

"I must applaud his timing." Despite the rapid beating of her heart, Charumati managed a smile. "It is a pity that he will not get an opportunity to rest."

"It is an even bigger pity that we had to ask him to come under such circumstances. It has hardly been a week since he got married."

Charumati looked shocked. She had not been aware of this. "His wife must be distraught. How much trouble I have caused to everyone!"

"Please do not berate yourself, Princess. Protecting the honour of a woman is one of the most important duties of a Rajput. Ratan Singh and I are merely performing that duty." The Rana paused. He carefully placed the sword on the diwan and then turned back to Charumati. Cupping her face in his hands, he slowly leaned forward and gently kissed her on the forehead. Charumati closed her eyes. If only time could stop here, now. She wanted to savour this moment. But time was not a luxury they had any more. Time was scarce, for the clock was ticking.

The Rana pulled back, and Charumati sighed. Taking his hand in hers, she whispered, "How I wish I could...."

"Trust me, even if you could turn back time, I doubt very much that you would do anything much differently. You are a Rajputain. No fear, no hesitation, and certainly no regrets."

He squeezed her hand and bent down to retrieve his sword from the diwan.

"The Rajguru is waiting to commence the puja. I must go now. But before I do, I have to entrust you with a responsibility. May I?"

"Anything Rana ji. Anything at all."

"I want you to carefully study each wall in this palace. So that you may find the perfect spot for that painting of Lord Krishna and Rukmani. If you recall, I had told you that I would only take that painting after I have honoured my promise. Well, the first thing that I will do after we win this war and return will be to accept the painting from you. Have faith, my Princess. That day is not far."

With that, the Rana turned and strode out of the bedroom.

Folding her hands, Charumati sighed and murmured softly to herself, "Protect him Bhavani Ma. Please protect this honourable man who I love more than my own life. This man who is now about to step into the *ranbhoomi* for me. This brave, fearless son of yours. Please protect him, Ma. Protect him."

***

Outside, the sky was azure dotted with specks of buttery gold and pale pink. The sun was still only partly visible, as it started its daily ascent from behind a crescent-shaped hill on the eastern side of the horizon. Udaipur and its surrounding farmlands were wrapped in a thin veil of dewy mist. Every morning, the country roads would resonate with the first sounds that heralded the beginning of a new day. The cowherds guiding their cattle along the coarse paths. The tinkle of lac bangles worn by the local women on their way to fill water from the nearest baoli. The grunting of camels, those beasts of burden with their humped backs piled high with goods of all kinds.

That day, however, there was nothing usual about the morning. The streets were eerily quiet, the absence of the cowherds and their cattle starkly noticeable. Trade and transportation had temporarily ceased. Every town, every village, every home in Mewar, was aware of the fact that Shahjahanabad had declared war on them. The arrival of the Mughal army had understandably come as a surprise to many, particularly given the peace offering that had arrived just a few days ago. Nevertheless, what was not astonishing was the preparedness of the Rajput force. Anyone would have thought that the army had been readying itself for a long time, but every Mewari knew that Mewar's force was, in fact, always ready for war. Given the turbulence that the state had countered for centuries and the fact that it was one of the very few that had successfully resisted Mughal domination over the years, their promptness of action should have come as no surprise to anyone.[87]

Now the children and women from the neighbouring towns and villages had been provided shelter in the forts, many of which had been built in the hilly parts of the region. The gates had been secured, and the storehouses had been well stocked with grains, pulses and other essentials. Requests for providing reinforcements had been sent to all the other Rajput states. There were, of course, several who would not oblige, either due to their allegiance with Shahjahanabad or because of their reluctance to anger the Mughal emperor. The ones who did support, however, did so whole-heartedly. For these valiant kings, it was a sense of collective Rajput pride that was above everything else, even their own survival. The glory of Mewar had been attacked, and this was the perfect time to come together and show the enemy its place.

A thundering sound suddenly reverberated around the silent streets of Udaipur, the echoes resonating through the rugged Aravalli hills that surrounded the city. The sound was much like the one that had awakened Charumati in the wee hours of that morning, only this time, it was moving in the opposite direction. For a few moments, though, nothing could be seen. Then, almost instantly, the horizon seemed to change colour as a mass of triangular crimson flags filled it. The sun on the flag was representative of the Suryavanshi maharanas or the sun dynasty of the state, and the *katar* or dagger was the emblem of independence for the defenders. And just like that, within seconds, the streets were teeming with horses, elephants, cannons and, of course, men. Thousands and thousands of them, all dressed in the uniform of the Rajput military, the same crimson as the colour of the flags they proudly carried. Each man wielded a gleaming sword smeared with a red tilak in his right hand and a shield in his left.

And right in front, sitting atop a white Malani horse, was Rana Raj Singh. Most of his predecessors had fought their battles on elephants, but Raj Singh, just like Maharana Pratap, rode a Malani horse. The horse's inward curving ears were a distinctive feature of the Malani breed of horses. Historically used as cavalry horses by the rulers of Marwar and Mewar, the Malani breed was famed for its bravery and loyalty. This one was no different. In fact, he came from a bloodline that had been bred by the royal family for generations. Now, just like the Rana riding him, the horse too seemed to be raring to get to the battlefield. His sleek white body was covered in armour, and he held his head high, proud to be leading the thousands that followed. And, as the sounds of the horses' hooves grew louder, and the elephants trumpeted louder still, it all finally rose to a deafening crescendo. Then, almost as though the gods themselves were showering their blessings on the marching men, the sky suddenly came alive with a magnificent burst of rose and marigold petals.

"Jai Bhavani!"

"Jai Bhavani!"

"Jai Bhavani!"

From the terraces of the forts, the voices of countless women and children came together as they collectively hailed the Rajput army. This was immediately followed by the perfectly synchronized tolling of temple bells from all around the city. It was believed that the sound vibrations would eliminate all negativity and open doors for a victorious future.

The sun suddenly burst out from behind the hills, dispersing its golden light all over the horizon. The morning sun was always a dazzling sight in Udaipur, but today it was as if the sun had come out in all its glory, to bestow its endless energy on its descendants, the Suryavanshis.

"Jai Bhavani, Jai Bhavani!"

As the voices of the striding men joined those of their womenfolk in a final war cry, it now seemed as though the entire city was there, saluting, upholding a legacy. It was the same legacy that Rana Kumba had defended when he'd defeated Mahmud Khalji in the Battle of Malwa. The legacy that Rana Sanga had protected when he'd fought and won eighteen pitched battles against the Sultans of Delhi, Malwa and Gujarat. The legacy that Maharana Pratap had inherited and upheld throughout his life. And it was the same legacy that Raj Singh was now going to defend. The legacy, the birthright to protect their homeland or die doing it.

Chapter 20

Enormous golden clouds rose into the air, enveloping the tranquil landscape into a turbulent mist of swirling sand. Stirred up by the hooves of thousands of galloping horses, it was almost as though a storm had arrived, momentarily shrouding the vision of the army waiting on the other side. Their instinctive reaction was to raise their hands to cover their faces, for the armour they wore covered everything but the eyes.

"Look at the speed of those horses," murmured one of the soldiers to another. "It is almost as though the men riding them are possessed by something so much bigger than a war."

"Trust me, they are," said the other man. He tightened his grip on his sword. They were in the front line and would be among the first to attack. "This is Mewar. They worship their swords like deities. This is not merely a war for them. This is their dharma. A matter of duty and honour."

"And for us, it is a matter of prestige," Diler Khan, sitting atop an elephant covered with armour, spoke in a firm tone. "No one insults the Mughal emperor and gets away. We have ruled this subcontinent for a hundred and thirty-four years.[88] We did not do that by staring in rapt admiration at the enemy. Speaking of which, here they come. Look sharp!"

The Rajputs had now assembled on the opposite side. Even as the two armies stood there, facing each other, Diler Khan drew and anchored his bow. Taking careful aim, he released the string. The arrow shot out. It raced through the air for a couple of seconds before landing precisely where it was intended to, inches away from the feet of the Rajput flag bearer. One of the cavalrymen jumped down from his horse. Removing the scroll from the end of the arrow, he handed it to Raj Singh.

Raj Singh opened the scroll. A final warning to hand Princess Charumati over and the threat to face the consequences at the failure to do so, had been written on it in a neat and legible handwriting.

With a grim expression, Raj Singh turned to his right. He didn't speak, instead he simply handed the scroll over to his friend, Ratan Singh Chundawat, who took it and without a moment's hesitation, set the scroll on fire with the flaming torch he held in his other hand. Within seconds, the scroll was reduced to ashes that fell to the ground in a crumbling grey mass. It was evidently clear what the Rajputs thought of the warning that had been issued to them.

Diler Khan was outraged at the blatant audacity of the Rajputs. To reject a warning or a threat was one thing, to burn it to cinders in full public view was no less than an insult. Clenching his right hand in a tight fist, he raised it and roared, "*Abu al-Muzaffar Muhi-ad-Din Muhammad Bahadur Alamgir Aurangzeb Badshah Zindabaad!*"

The thousands of Mughal soldiers present there immediately joined in, collectively echoing the last words of their general. Several of them held the official imperial *alam* in their hands and even as they hailed their emperor, they lifted their arms and raised the flags with palpable pride.

"Zindabad, Zindabad!"

"Alamgir Aurangzeb Badshah Zindabad!"

Raj Singh drew his sword and raised it high above his head. "Jai Bhavani!" he thundered in turn. "*Aakramaan ke liye taiyaar!*"

The sound of blowhorns and drums suddenly reverberated around the open battlefield. Used by warring forces around the world since time immemorial, this was the official signal of the commencement of war.

Instantly, the soldiers on both sides drew their swords. Thrusting their shields in front of them, they assumed their positions. The neighing horses stamped their feet. The elephants lifted their trunks, trumpeting loudly.

"*Sipahiyon! Ghur Savaar! Aakramaan!*"

At Raj Singh's words, hundreds of Rajput soldiers and cavalrymen advanced toward the enemy. From the opposing side, the Mughals dashed forward too. Even as the two sides charged ahead in one perfectly synchronized movement, the majestic Aravalli hills and glorious sand dunes created a magnificent backdrop, almost making it look like a war scene from a work of art by a talented court artist. Of course, this was not a painting or a sketch that could be presented to an emperor or hung on a wall in the palace of a raja. This was the beginning of a war. A beginning that would transform the pristine golden sand to a crimson ocean within moments. Glistening swords soaked in blood, soldiers lunging forward knowing there was no return, severed legs and arms strewn around in abundance, elephants trumpeting as they stamped the life out of half dead men. Nothing was too much, for this was a war for honour, prestige, love and revenge. Monumental in its breadth, colossal in its repercussions, this war between two of the mightiest empires of the Indian subcontinent would go on to determine not only the fate of a brave and beautiful Rajput Princess but also the destiny and future of the two empires fighting it.

***

If Sahal ardently worshipped the rising sun, she found the setting sun equally mesmerizing. To many, it might have been a melancholic scene, but Sahal had always thought that there was something otherworldly about a sunset, the way it changed colour from golden to red, dispersing light all over the horizon, casting the entire sky with a resplendent ruby glow. Then it seemed to grow larger and larger, before finally beginning its steady descent behind a hillock on the western side.

"It is called *Surya* from rising to setting and *Savitr* from setting to rising. According to the *Rig Veda*, 'Savitr' means 'sending to sleep'. That, my dear, is the true meaning of a sunset," Sahal's aunt had once told her.

And with it, the world too seemed to go to sleep. The birds would fly back to their nests, the cowherds would gather their cattle and trudge back down the hills. Mothers would call to their children to return home. As for Sahal, she was content to simply stand by her window and witness the magic every evening.

That evening too, she was watching it from her bedroom window when there was a knock at her door. With a sigh, Sahal pulled herself away from the sunset. "Come in," she called out.

It was her personal daasi. "A letter has come for you, Rani sa," she informed Sahal. "The messenger awaits an answer."

Sahal didn't need to ask who had sent it. Weeks had passed since the war had begun and the pile of letters just kept growing. They had been coming at regular intervals since the day he'd departed, so many of them, far too many. And they all contained the same message. Perhaps it would be wrong to call it a message. It was so much more than that. It was a longing, a yearning. A lamentation of being separated from your love, of the pain that came as a result of that separation.

Sahal took the letter from the daasi and opened it. A Rajputain is not supposed to bare her grief in the presence of anyone, but this was one time Sahal could not stop herself. Instant tears formed in her eyes almost as soon as she saw her husband's handwriting and then read his first words. Gasping, she had to clasp a hand to her mouth to keep herself from crying out.

I miss you, my love. I miss you so much that it hurts in a way I never thought possible. I never imagined that I would care so much, love so deeply. Sometimes it seems unbearable, this separation. How can I go on like this? How can I stay away from you, tear my mind away from thoughts that are impossible to resist? They say the stench of death is unendurable here, but all I can smell is the delicate aroma of the kesar chandan perfume you apply each morning after your bath. They say that the sounds of guns and cannons pierce their ears all the time, but all I can hear is the sound of your melodious voice. They tell me that the heat is becoming more and more unbearable with each passing day, but all I can feel is the waft of cool air that blows when you sit with me at dinner each evening and wave the pankha back and forth so that I may eat in comfort. Sahal, your presence fills my being, even when we're away from each other. So much so that sometimes I almost feel as though I can touch your face, weave my fingers through your hair, listen to the sounds of your breathing as I lie here in my tent, night after night, counting the weeks, the days, the hours, the minutes.

I am doing my duty, my love. This duty that is my dharma, this duty that you wanted me to perform. But not a minute, not a second, passes when I do not think of you. Keep me in your thoughts as I keep you in mine. Remember that I love you more than you can ever imagine. And now, I must ask you for something.

Send me a memento, Sahal. Do not let my messenger return empty-handed. Give him a token, something, anything that will remind me of you. I will keep it close to me and ride into the battlefield. And then surely, we will win this war and be together again.

The last words had blurred in front of Sahal's eyes, for the tears were now pouring down. She had her back to the daasi, but the girl did not need to see her face to sense the intensity of her grief. Helpless, she watched Sahal's shoulders heaving as she sobbed silently. How do you comfort a newly married woman who has sent her husband off to the battlefield only seven days after their marriage? How do you even begin to try to tell her that everything will be all right when her husband has gone off to fight one of the hardest battles of his life?

Several minutes passed. The daasi gently touched Sahal on the shoulder. "Rani sa?"

Wiping her tears with the end of her odhni, Sahal turned. Her eyes were still moist, but the expression on her face had changed. What was it? Determination? Resignation? Courage? The daasi could not tell.

"Thank you, Bhago. You may leave now and come back in an hour. In the meantime, please meet the messenger and tell him that I will have a response for him shortly."

"Allow me to stay with you, Rani sa," pleaded the daasi. "Please do not ask to be left alone at a time like this."

"No. I want to be alone. I *need* to be alone. Please come back in an hour," repeated the queen firmly.

"But Rani sa—"

"Ekaant!"

There was nothing more to be said. Bowing her head, the daasi left the room. Once she had closed the door and the sound of her retreating footsteps had waned, Sahal walked back to the window. The letter from Ratan Singh was still clutched tight in her hand. As she looked out of the jaali, she saw that the sun had almost vanished by then. Just a muted red sliver remained. Sahal watched it for a few minutes until that too had disappeared from her sight, slipping behind the hills.

Light suddenly flooded the room once again. For a moment, Sahal couldn't fathom where it had come from, and she blinked in surprise. Then she realized that it was time to light the evening *mashaals*. One by one they were lit, the long iron torches burning bright, radiating enough light so that Sahal could unfold her husband's letter and read it one last time.

When the daasi returned an hour later, Sahal was wearing the vermillion red poshak she had donned on her wedding day. Her ghoonghat though, ensured that she remained oblivious to the look of astonishment that appeared on the woman's face when she saw Sahal dressed like that. It did cross her mind that the queen might have momentarily lost her senses or become delusional. Intense worry about a loved one or the grief of being separated from them often did that to people.

"Rani sa," Folding her hands, the daasi bowed to Sahal. "The messenger awaits your response."

"Yes. I am to give him a memento for my husband. He wants me to send something that he can carry with him into the battlefield so that he may feel my presence at all times."

"Ji Hukum."

"I have been worried since the first letter came. I cannot help but feel that he is constantly thinking about me, and that the distraction is keeping him from doing his best in this *dharma yudh*. This last letter has confirmed that I am correct."

A crease appeared on the daasi's forehead as she tried to fathom the tenor of finality that had suddenly surfaced in Sahal's voice. And why was she calling it a 'last letter'?

"Rani sa, I...."

"Bhago, you have served me tirelessly since the day I came here. It would not be an exaggeration to say that you have been nothing but wonderful to me. Even today. You have been the bearer of this letter that my husband has written to me. I cannot even begin to express what that means to me..." Sahal paused. The daasi waited.

Several minutes passed before she spoke again. "The task I am now about to give you is not going to be easy to carry out. But I know that you will do it with the utmost sincerity."

"This kingdom is my *annadaata,* Rani sa." The daasi looked at Sahal earnestly. "I would gladly give up my life for it."

"Your loyalty is unquestionable, Bhago. That is why I am entrusting you with this. As requested by my husband, I am sending him something that will allow him to feel my presence. But it is also something that will ensure that he no longer feels pressured, distracted or diverted from his duty. From this moment onwards, he will focus only on winning this war. Please ensure that it is taken to my husband. Along with this letter."

She handed a sealed envelope to the daasi. Even as she took the letter, she couldn't help wondering about the memento. What was the Rani going to give her? A pendant? A ring? A lock of her hair?

Suddenly Sahal turned around and walked toward the wall on the left side of the room. This wall held an ornamental display of shields and swords, all different styles, shapes and sizes. Each sword that had been exhibited on the wall had a history of its own. Without a moment's hesitation, Sahal pulled out a straight, double-edged sword with a gilded pommel. There was an urgency to her movements, as though contemplation or delay might change her mind.

"This is the memento. Please have it delivered to my husband at once."

Then, before the daasi could even think about stopping her, Sahal veered the sword toward herself and in one sharp, swift swing, from left to right, sliced it right through her own neck.[89] The astounded daasi watched in shocked disbelief as the queen's head tilted to the right, first a little, then more, and ultimately separated from the neck and dropped down. Darting forward, the daasi was able to move fast enough to gather the head in her extended hands before Sahal's body finally slumped to the floor. The blood that began to pour out, rapidly covered the pristine white of the marble, forming a crimson pool that matched the colour of the poshak she was wearing.

On hearing the daasi's screams, scores of people quickly gathered in the room. Members of the royal family, ministers, royal guards, *khansamas*, attendants, even the messenger who had been waiting for the response, they all stood there staring at the headless body of the queen in mute shock. Soon the shocked silence gave way to speculative whispers as they tried to make sense of what had happened. How could someone as young and beautiful as her do this? What had the motivation been? Yes, she had been melancholic since Ratan Singh had gone to war. The letters had been coming in consistently, but had she spoken to anyone about them? Had anyone seen this coming? What news had the messenger brought today?

Then the daasi who still looked visibly shaken, managed to compose herself enough to tell the family how the queen had wept on reading her husband's letter and then dismissed her because she wished to be on her own. "She felt that he was unable to concentrate on the war because of her. She thought she was an obstacle to his doing his duty toward his homeland," she said between racking sobs. "And so, she sacrificed herself."

Afterwards, a golden plate was brought and Bhago carefully placed the head on it. Wiping her eyes, she handed the plate to the messenger. "It was the queen's last wish to deliver this to her beloved husband. Please take this to the chieftain along with the queen's letter. And ensure that you do so in time. Her sacrifice must not be in vain."

The messenger took the plate from the daasi and got ready to leave. Soon, the body would be bathed and wrapped in a clean white cloth. Then a priest would sprinkle holy water on it. The body would be placed on the pyre while the priest chanted the ceremonial hymns. The queen had no children so a close male relative would set the pyre alight, while the mourners present at the funeral would weep. Of course, the ritual of pouring holy water into the mouth of the deceased could not be performed in this case.

"I had heard endless tales about her valour and fearlessness," the messenger said to Bhaago as he turned back to look at the body on the floor. "She was kind, generous, humane and a great swordswoman as well. People who had seen her engage in talwar baazi often claimed that along with being quick and nimble, Rani sa also had a keen sense of timing, distance measure and most importantly, decisiveness."

The daasi nodded sadly. "Well, that I can certainly vouch for. Even today, she was quick, nimble and her sense of timing and distance were spot on. And when she walked up to that wall and picked up the sword, it was evident to me that she had made a decision and was most certainly going to carry it out."

With bowed head, the messenger then carried the plate bearing the queen's head, out of the room. Even as the daasi watched him leave, she knew one thing for certain. Never would she ever be able to erase from her mind what she had just witnessed.

CHAPTER 21

At first sight, the horizon looked overcast, as though it would start pouring with rain any moment. On careful observation, however, it was clear that the grey pallor of the sky did not hold the sweet promise of rain. Rain that would fall and drench the parched, cracked earth that looked like it hadn't received a drop in a very long time. This grey instead had an ashen quality to it, the colour perfectly in sync with the sounds of the bombs and gunfire that had gone on ceaselessly for weeks now.

"It is always astounding to me how quickly our ears get used to the sounds," said Raj Singh to Ratan Singh one day. They were sitting in Ratan Singh's tent, planning the strategy for the next morning.

"Humans are naturally adaptive creatures. Put them anywhere and they learn how to survive."

Raj Singh looked at Ratan. There was a palpably distracted tone in his voice. He looked preoccupied too, as though his thoughts were somewhere faraway. But he had been that way ever since this war had started. Most of the time, when he was not on the field, he was in his tent, either staring at nothing in particular, or quietly writing a letter. Raj Singh was aware of the fact that several letters had in fact, already been sent to Salumbar. Each of the letters had also promptly received an answer. Not for the first time, Raj Singh felt a pang of guilt at calling upon his friend at such an inopportune time. Forcing a smile, he patted Ratan Singh on the hand.

"I am pleased to see that several kingdoms have supported us by sending reserve forces. It has provided a much needed relief to our soldiers."

"Yes, though I have to admit that Man Singh's force was the biggest surprise of them all." Ratan Singh shook his head in disbelief. "At first, I thought he might be trying to deceive us, but now I can see the sincerity with which they are backing us in the battlefield. I cannot help but wonder what made him turn over to our side."

"I think he was simply too frightened to stand up to the emperor on his own. Now that he can see how much support we have garnered, he is not scared anymore. In any case, whatever his motivation and reasons, it is certainly heartening news for Princess Charumati. She will be ecstatic to know that her brother is now standing firmly by our side to protect and honour her."

"She will be even more ecstatic once we defeat the enemy and this war ends," said Ratan Singh.

"How are the food supplies? I heard they are running thin." A crease of worry appeared on the Rana's forehead.

"It is not particularly alarming at this point. Though we might want to take stock soon."

"And the morale of the men? We have to take care of that as well. It is not easy to fight a war like this in the scorching heat of the desert."

"That is never a concern with our men. Just watching you, being led by you, is the greatest motivation for them."

"You are far too humble." Raj Singh shook his head. "We are lucky to have you with us. You are the finest example of Rajput valour, my friend."

"Hukum? Hukum?"

The Rana instantly became alert at the sound of the familiar voice. "Manik Lal?" he called out. "Is that you? Come into the tent. Ratan and I are both here."

The flap opened. Bending slightly, for he was tall, Manik Lal entered the tent. He then bowed to both the men before turning to Ratan Singh.

"Hukum, the messenger has returned from Salumbar. He has brought a letter and a memento for you. Would you care to meet him now?"

"Of course!" The chieftain stood up at once. "Please send him right away."

"Well then, we will leave you to it, Ratan." Raj Singh rose to leave. "I am sure you would like some privacy."

Followed by Manik Lal, he walked out of the tent. Even as he passed the waiting messenger, he noticed that the man was carefully holding a golden plate in both hands. The plate was almost completely covered with a satin cloth so that only its rim was visible. Nodding to the man to go in, Raj Singh strode on. The alertness on his face and the confidence of his stride effectively concealed the fatigue he felt, for he had not slept a wink in two days. He knew that even though Ratan Singh and he had discussed the problem of food scarcity, if there was one thing that was truly a precious resource and always precariously in short supply during a war, it was sleep. Raj Singh rubbed his tired eyes. It would be good to use this time and get a couple of hours of rest, now that he had the opportunity. Sighing in exhaustion, he was just turning in the direction of his own tent on the other side of the barracks, when a deafening anguished roar suddenly reverberated around the entire camp. So full of pain was the sound that it was obvious that it had been made by someone in great distress.

The Rana looked at Manik Lal in astonishment. "What was that? Did I imagine it, or did that sound actually come from Ratan Singh's tent?"

"Ji Hukum. It certainly seems to have come from there." Manik Lal looked as stunned. "What could have caused it? The messenger just went in and...."

Raj Singh did not give him the time to finish. Turning on his heel, he dashed toward Ratan Singh's tent, but had barely covered half the distance when the flap of the tent was thrown open and Ratan Singh appeared. The Rana stared at his friend. From the expression on his face, it was evident that something terrible had happened. The man looked crazed, his eyes wild with grief. And what was that around his neck? Was it... no no... it couldn't be....

"Manik Lal?" Raj Singh's voice had fallen to a precautious whisper. "Is that..."

He could not even bring himself to complete the sentence.

Both men stood there, gaping, rooted to the spot as they tried to make sense of what was happening. Other soldiers gathered, silent and speculative.

A few moments passed before Manik Lal lowered his eyes and nodded, confirming what the Rana could clearly see. "Ji Hukum. It seems as though the Queen of Salumbar has sent her severed head to her husband as a memento. He has tied her head around his neck with the hair."

"But why did she do something like that?" Raj Singh felt as though his entire body had become numb. He just could not bring himself to move. "Why Manik Lal? I cannot understand."

"He missed her so dreadfully, so incessantly. Perhaps she believed she was distracting him from the battlefield, keeping him from performing his duty." Manik Lal shook his head. "It is no wonder that he seems to have lost his mind with grief."

Unable to move an inch forward to comfort his friend in this terrible moment, unable to face him, to even properly fathom what was happening, Raj Singh watched helplessly as Ratan Singh suddenly turned and walked away. For a panicked moment, he thought that Ratan might be about to do something to himself, but the chieftain returned within seconds, his horse in tow. Mounting the stallion, he climbed onto its back. The severed head of Sahal Kanwar was still secured around his neck. Grabbing the reins of the horse with one hand, Ratan drew his sword with the other.

"Jai Bhavani!" he bellowed, his voice resonating with all the pain, all the anguish, all the rage that he was feeling. His war cry seemed to snap Raj Singh out of his stupor, and he reeled forward with extended arms toward his friend. Ratan Singh, though, was not going to be held back now. His eyes glistening brightly with unshed tears, he lowered his head and looked at the memento his beloved wife had sent for him.

"I promise you, Sahal," he murmured then. "I pledge that I will not let your sacrifice be in vain. This war for which you gave up your life, we will win this war. We will."

Then, before anyone could stop him, he pulled the horse's reins, steered it to the left and galloped off into the battlefield.[90]

***

The rest he had been craving earlier, didn't come easily to the Rana that night. He lay in his tent, tossing and turning for hours, going over the details of the day's events in his mind. He knew he wasn't the only one. Every man in the barracks was distraught about what had happened. Aware of the fact that sleep would continue to be elusive that night, he finally threw off his *razai* and got up. His writing paper and instruments were in a leather pouch on the side of the tent. Opening the pouch, he got what he needed and settled down. He hadn't written her as many letters as Ratan had sent to his wife, but now he felt the need to communicate with her. As he put the quill to paper, he realized that even though he needed to write to her, he didn't want to tell her about the terrible tragedy that had occurred that day. For one thing, he knew his hands would not stay steady if he so much as tried to describe the event in words, and for another, he simply did not want to burden her with the heartbreaking news. He knew she was constantly praying for him, for the victory of their force, and the last thing he wanted to do was to shake her faith. So, he wrote instead about the valour of their men and how they were fighting the war with every ounce of might. He related to her how the other kingdoms had supported them by sending reinforcements, strengthening their belief in Rajput solidarity.

Your brother and his force are unequivocally in this with us now, he wrote. *Admittedly, his presence has given me heart.*

He then went on to tell her about life in the barracks and how different the two encampments were.

To say the Mughals are elaborate in their travel arrangements would be an understatement. Their camp is almost like a city in itself. They are, however, finding it hard to adjust to life here. But then, that is hardly surprising. Life in the desert is harsh. The days are so hot that it sometimes feels as if the landscape will burst into flames. The nights though, are beautiful. The sky turns into a canvas glimmering with magical stardust. The stars seem brighter here, the moon more luminous than ever. And the music! It is sublime for as soon as the sun goes down, a special concert begins. The coyotes, the crickets, the cicadas, they all come together like a splendid symphony of notes, and I have to admit that I often lie here in my tent, listening in wonder.

"I did not realize that a warrior like you could be so romantic." It was almost as though he could hear her voice, teasing him as she had done when he had brought her to Udaipur. Pausing, he closed his eyes. Images of her lovely face ran through his mind as he remembered the first time he had seen her at his coronation. She might have thought that he hadn't noticed her, but how could he have not? She had undoubtedly been the most beautiful woman there. Those dark brown lotus shaped eyes that flitted here and there as they took in the scene, the delicate fingers that clutched the odhni to make sure it wouldn't slip, the slightly haughty pout of her lips that revealed a pride that most Rajputains were known to possess. She had attended the ceremony with her father, and Raj Singh had glimpsed her as she stood there, glancing at him coyly from behind her ghoonghat. Their eyes hadn't met, but he knew she'd been looking at him. And he'd smiled and promised himself that one day, when the right time came, he would ask for her hand in marriage. Fate, though, obviously had other plans for never in his wildest dreams could he have imagined that a day would come when she would write to him herself. But she had. And how far they had come from that coronation!

Raj Singh opened his eyes and pulled himself back to the present. He picked up the quill and pressed it to the paper again.

It has been several weeks, but it feels more like months. Months since I awoke to the sound of the morning aarti in Jag mandir. Months since I listened to the call of the peacocks perched on the highest terraces of the Raj Mahal. And months since I watched your beautiful face as you sit and admire the reflection of the palace in the shimmering waters of Lake Pichola. But....

The quill lingered over the paper for a few seconds as he wondered whether to share with her what he had been feeling. After all, it was what his heart was telling him. And it was his firm belief that the heart never lies.

Fret not Princess, because this will all be over soon, he wrote. *I believe, I know, that this war will end before much longer. Yes, this war will end, Mewar will emerge victorious, and then I will return to Raj Mahal. And to you.*

Chapter 22

Some of the earlier Mughals had found the soaring temperatures in India difficult to bear. So much so that they took it upon themselves to find a solution to the relentless heat by using skilful water engineering techniques like channelling cooling water using covered waterways.[91] Babur, in fact, dedicated an entire chapter to this in his *Tuzk-e-Babri* or *Baburnama*. However, those who had been born in India, like Aurangzeb, acclimatized to the heat much more easily. It was not surprising then that even on a hot day like this, Aurangzeb preferred to sit outdoors to eat his meals. A *shamiana* set up by the staff in a shaded spot near the river bank, was sufficient for him as he sat there on the *dastarkhwan*, enjoying a meal of *qubooli* and *panchmel dal*. The qubooli had been made using the best quality Bengal gram, apricots and almonds.[92] Each grain of rice was coated with silver varq and the food had been tasted by an official of the royal kitchen to ensure its safety before being served to the emperor. As always, the meal had been preceded by the emperor doing *bismillah*.

"Those are his favourite dishes. Perhaps I should let him complete his meal." Zeb-un-Nissa glanced at Jai Singh. They were watching him from a distance, wondering whether to approach him right away. It was usually unheard of to disturb the emperor in the middle of a meal.

"He will want to know. He will be furious if he learns that we withheld the information from him, even for a short while." Jai Singh sighed. "I would have told him but given the circumstances...."

"I understand, Mirza Raja."

Zeb knew that she was one of the very few who could be completely candid with the emperor. "I will break the news to him myself. And you are right. It is not wise to keep this to ourselves any longer."

She crossed the distance quickly, and her father looked up from his meal as he saw his daughter approach. Noticing that the frown on his forehead had deepened, Zeb felt her heartbeat beginning to race. She had been dreading this moment ever since the news had reached her.

"What are you doing here at this time, Zeb? You know I do not like company at meals." Aurangzeb always ate his meals alone.

"I am sorry, Father. I would never have intruded on your time like this. But the news I bring cannot wait."

"And whose *darkhwast* do you bring to me this time?" Aurangzeb shook his head. "When will you tire of performing these good deeds, dear daughter? In any case, I am not in the mood to be very forgiving today."

Zeb knew that this was not the time to mince words or beat around the bush. She took a deep breath.

"Our army has been forced to retreat from Udaipur, Father. Mirza Raja has just received the news. What remains of the force is on its way back to Delhi."

The emperor stopped eating. He was silent for a few minutes before he finally raised his head and nodded slowly. "I see. Returning to Delhi. Empty-handed once more."

"I am afraid so, Father." Zeb bowed her head.

"To overcome the Mughal army in an open encounter. To force a ferocious man like Diler Khan to retreat." His voice was dangerously low to Zeb's ears.

"Father, please! I...."

Aurangzeb closed his eyes briefly. "I agreed to all his demands during the war of succession. I gave him mahals, parganas, the status he wanted. I even gave him the opportunity of a last warning when he ambushed our forces and killed our men. This time, though, Raj Singh has gone too far."

"Father, there is no point now. We might as well accept...."

He opened his eyes suddenly and Zeb-un-Nissa blinked in shock. Furious, piercing, those eyes seemed to have turned to fire within seconds.

"Accept? Accept!"

Uncrossing his legs, Aurangzeb rose from the dastarkhwan.

"You should know me well enough, daughter!" He directly addressed Zeb then. "I rarely forget, and I never forgive. And one thing I can tell you is that this has most certainly soured our relations with Raj Singh and Mewar. For a long time to come. And speaking of souring, the Bengal gram used in the qubooli was far too rancid for my taste today."

Zeb-un-Nissa stared at him with a thumping heart. Aurangzeb's voice had risen considerably and from where he stood, Jai Singh could hear every word clearly. The general and Zeb exchanged a look. They were both well aware that this was not a simple change of subject.

"The head khansama and every single member of the royal kitchen who helped prepare that qubooli will be tried in court tomorrow. They will each receive lashings as per the part they have played in preparing the dish. Furthermore, the head khansama will be banished from the kingdom!"

He began striding out, but then turned around to look at Zeb one last time. "Do not worry, Zeb. I am sure destiny will bring Raj Singh and I face to face at some point in the future. After all, as is stated in the *Baburnama,* 'What though the field be lost, all is not lost. The unconquerable will and courage, Never submit or yield.'"

The news soon spread like wildfire around the palace. Disbelief, fury, speculation, the reactions were plenty and varied. In a matter of hours, it seemed as though every person in Shahjahanabad was whispering and talking about it. There were those who were staunchly loyal to the emperor and the throne and couldn't stop shaking their heads that the blasphemy hadn't been meted out the correct justice. Then there were some who had been secretly sympathetic toward Charumati and were glad at the outcome. And in the midst of it all, was a brave Rajputain, the one who had risked her life for this. Even as the others discussed and mused over the events of the last few months down to the minutest detail, Jodhpuri Begum observed it all like a silent spectator, listening, understanding, inwardly rejoicing. Her manner though, gave nothing away as she watched with an impassive expression. It was only when she walked into the chamber late that night that she allowed the slightest hint of a smile to cross her face. The chamber that had been readied for Charumati's arrival and now lay vacant and silent. Jodhpuri looked around. The grand arched doorway with its red and white minarets, the extensive courtyard and garden, the multiple rooms furnished with priceless jewels, silks, gold and silver, the marble bath with its domed skylight. It was indeed one of the most spectacular chambers in the harem.

"How fortunate you are, Charumati!" exclaimed Jodhpuri to herself. "This beautiful chamber was made to imprison you, hold you captive. Here, in the heart of all this beauty, you would have surely wilted, withered away. Now, never shall you ever inhabit it. And even as you go on to lead a wonderful new life with the Rana, this chamber shall stay vacant, empty, a constant reminder of this monumental event that will remain etched in our memories forever."

Pausing, she folded her hands. Her lips moved in a silent prayer of gratitude as she thanked Bhavani Ma for bestowing her blessings. And then, as quietly as she had come, she left the chamber and returned to her own rooms. Tonight, after a long time, she would sleep peacefully.

***

The following day, Charumati awoke to the sound of rain. It had started off as a light drizzle in the wee hours, but had advanced to a gentle, steady shower by mid-morning. Now, the Princess sat by the window in her bedroom in Raj Mahal, watching the falling drops. Down in the central courtyard, a pride of peacocks had collected, their vivid feathered tails opened into perfect semi-circular fans as they cavorted and pranced around.

"All that strutting and frolicking just to attract a mate," said Nirmal, rolling her eyes. "And will you look at that one! Vanity personified!"

Charumati smiled at Nirmal. She had arrived in Udaipur with the force that had come from Kishengarh and had dashed straight to the palace. The journey had been well worth it for Charumati's eyes had lit up instantly at the sight of her friend. They'd rushed into each other's arms, and it had felt to both women as though they hadn't met in years.

"Well, considering that peahens often choose a male solely on the basis of the quality of their trains, I suppose all that hard work is justified," Charu said.

"The scene down there reminds me of that day." Nirmal rested her chin on the palm of her right hand and peered down. "The rain, the dancing peacocks!"

Charu knew her friend was talking about that fateful afternoon in Kishengarh when the old woman with the paintings had visited their palace. How quickly the time had passed. "I cannot believe so many months have gone by. Perhaps life will soon come full circle for us, Nirmal."

"I hope so, Charu. I really hope so."

Just then, there was a frantic knocking at the door. "Rajkumari sa! Nirmal sa! Can we come in?"

Charumati immediately recognized Ganga's voice. "Come in Ganga," she called out.

The bedroom door was flung open and half a dozen daasis burst into the room. Charu and Nirmal stared, astounded.

"What is going on?" started Charumati. "What are all of you doing here?"

"Rajkumari sa! It is about Hukum."

For an instant Charumati thought her heart would stop. The room spun around her even as she dashed forward and clutched Ganga's hands. "What happened to Rana ji? Is he all right? Where is he? Tell me fast!"

"He is on his way back to the palace with the force. The Mughals have retreated!"

Charumati stared at Ganga, not completely able to comprehend what she was hearing. "Retreated? That means...."

"Yes, Rajkumari sa! We have won the war! We have won! Rana ji is safe."

"Nirmal!" Whirling around, Charumati held her arms out to her friend and the two women stumbled into each other's embrace. They hugged, they laughed, not bothering to even wipe their eyes as tears of joy flowed down copiously.

"Hold me, Nirmal! Hold me! I might not be able to muster the strength to even stand."

Weak with relief, Charumati allowed Nirmal to gently prod her into the nearest chair even as the daasis stood by, some smiling, some quietly murmuring prayers of gratitude.

A few moments passed before another daasi stepped forward. "The welcome aarti, Rajkumari sa?" she asked. "Should I get it ready?"

"Of course!" Voice trembling with emotion, Charumati rose from the chair. "I want to do the aarti myself. And light up the entire palace with diyas! It should sparkle like never before when the Rana and the chieftain return with the force."

There was a short silence as the Princess waited for the daasis to respond. But they just stood there with bowed heads and lowered eyes. The smiles had faded as well, and Charumati finally addressed the one standing closest to her.

"What is it? Why this sudden hush? Surely, the palace has not fallen short of diyas, has it?" With a nervous laugh, she waved her hand toward the door. "Go now! The welcome has to be befitting of the victory."

"Rajkumari sa." Ganga stepped forward. "This is a day that will always be remembered, will be forever recalled for more reasons than one. For today is indeed a day that is as joyous as it is tragic. A day that is bittersweet, the triumph of victory marred by the heartbreak of loss."

"Loss?" Charumati looked at the daasi quizzically. "Mewar has won the war, the Rana is safe and on his way home. What are you talking about?"

"Ji, Rajkumari sa. You are correct. Today is the day Mewar and Rana ji have emerged victorious in one of the biggest battles they have had to fight. It is most certainly a reason to celebrate, to rejoice. Ironically, it is also a day to grieve, a day to mourn the loss of a great chieftain, a loyal friend, one of the bravest soldiers that Rajputana has ever known."

Seeing no point in withholding the terrible news, Ganga looked at the Princess with tears in her eyes. "Our Ranaji's dearest friend, the

Chundawat chieftain, Rawat Ratan Singh will not be returning for he is no more with us."

The Princess gasped. Feeling her legs go weak, she clutched at the mantelpiece for support. Just then, a sudden thunderous roar made them all jump as a streak of lightning lashed against the window. Nirmal noticed that the mild shower outside had now turned into an incessant downpour.

"Almost as if the skies themselves are mourning this tremendous loss." She put her arm around the princess's shoulder and asked the daasi. "How did this happen?"

Ganga then related the series of events that had led to this. How the newly married couple, so in love with each other, had pined silently as Ratan Singh tried to fulfil his duty and Sahal waited for him to return. How she, later convinced that thoughts of her were keeping him from fulfilling his dharma, took her own life and sent her severed head to him as a memento. "He tied his beloved's head around his neck and stormed into the battle," she recounted. "Eyewitnesses have said that it seemed as though he was crazed by pain and rage. He was unstoppable, and he fought like a man possessed by a sole aim. To ensure that Mewar emerges victorious and that his wife's sacrifice does not go in vain. And it really was his only wish because no sooner did the Mughals retreat, than the chieftain fell to the ground and cut off his own head.[93] Having lost the woman he loved, he also lost the desire to live. The war ended, and so did his life."

"A love story never ends." Nirmal looked around the room. Not a single eye was dry. Wiping her own, she said, "The lovers may be gone, but the story is eternal. The story of this brave Rajput king and his fearless queen, two people who loved each other more than anything else, yet gave up their lives for this war and for Mewar. They shall forever be remembered and hailed. Their story will be told far and wide, for decades, even centuries, long after you and me and all of us are gone."

She then turned toward Charumati. The Princess still looked visibly shocked and could just not stop crying. "Nirmal," she spoke between sobs. "How can I ever forget that this happened because of me? They gave up their lives to protect my honour and...."

"*Veergati.*" In spite of her own tears, Nirmal smiled. "The martyrdom that is the proud legacy of a Rajput. Ratan Singh and Sahal Kanwar are both martyrs. He fought in the battlefield until his last breath. For him, the honour and prestige of his homeland was above everything else, even his own life. She sacrificed hers for the same cause. They both did their duties and achieved veergati. Pray, let us not tarnish something that is sacrosanct with tears and regrets."

Nirmal then placed her hands on her friend's shoulders and shook her gently. "Pull yourself together Charu. The victorious force is on its way back. The welcome aarti must be performed."

Chapter 23

When Raj Singh and his army entered the palace gates, most of Udaipur's population had congregated there to welcome them. Dhols and nagaras were being played and the flag of Mewar had been hoisted at the gates. It now swayed to and fro in the gentle breeze that always followed a downpour. Charumati's brother, Man Singh, was there too, along with his force. Even as the men entered the gates and walked down the pathway, they were greeted with showers of marigold petals and calls of 'Rana ji ki jai! Rana ji ki jai!'

Raj Singh stopped and raised his right hand, palm facing the people. The shouts quietened immediately.

"Today we have returned victorious because of the love and faith that we have received from all of you. You have supported us in this enormous quest, our quest to uphold the honour of Mewar. This honour for which we live, for which we are ready to die." Raj Singh paused for a moment, then folded his hands.

"There are some who did die," he continued as his praja listened. "Those brave, fearless, courageous warriors who gave up their lives in this quest. Before you hail me, before you hail any of us here, hail them. Thank them. For their sacrifice is priceless, invaluable. The names of these martyrs shall be remembered always. And among them is my dearest friend Rawat Ratan Singh Chundawat and his queen Sahal Kanwar. We will commemorate this day of victory by acknowledging them first."

No sooner had he finished speaking, than countless voices rose and reverberated around the palace grounds in one unanimous call.

"Rawat Ratan Singh ki jai!"

"Rawat Ratan Singh ki jai!"

"Rani Sahal Kanwar ki jai!"

Even as the thousands gathered there hailed the martyrs, Raj Singh closed his eyes for a moment. "Ratan, my friend." His tone was soft, so much so that only he could hear his words. "You will be missed every day. Every single day. Mewar will never forget your sacrifice. Thank you for upholding everything that is dear to us. It was an honour and a privilege to fight this war with you by my side. Thank you."

And then, just for an instant, it was as though he could actually feel his friend's presence around him. The tall, strong, fearless, strapping chieftain of the Chundawat clan. He, who had gone to war seven days after his marriage. He, who had fought valiantly until the very end. He, who had died defending and upholding the honour of Mewar. And his queen. As brave, as fearless, as selfless. Without a moment's hesitation, gave up her life for her homeland. Their names would go down in the pages of history and keep the legacy alive. A legacy of truth, valour, tradition and sacrifice.

When Raj Singh opened his eyes, Manik Lal was standing next to him. "Are you all right, Hukum?" he asked, his brow creased with concern.

The Rana nodded. "Yes, I am." Then he looked at Manik Lal thoughtfully, the memory of their first meeting suddenly coming back to him. "Do you recall the first time we met in that forest, Manik Lal? Can you believe that I almost shot you with my bow and arrow that day? How far we have come from there!"

Manik Lal joined his hands and bowed to Raj Singh. "Thank you for believing in me, Hukum. I had lost my way, but you brought me back on the right path. My *Bapusa* and *Maasa* can hold their heads high with pride today, for their son is no longer a dacoit. He is now a proud member of the Mewar army." He looked up at the palace and then at the crowds of people gathered there. "This is like homecoming to me. This is where I belong."

Raj Singh hugged Manik Lal and then turned toward the palace entrance. A congregation of women stood there, waiting to perform the traditional welcome. And right in the middle of the group, holding the aarti, was the Princess. Smiling to himself, Raj Singh wondered at the irony of it. Only a few months ago, he had rescued her, bringing her to Udaipur with him. How frightened, how unsure she had been then! And now, here she was, at the entrance of Raj Mahal, waiting to welcome him back to the same palace where he had brought her.

Raj Singh started walking toward her. She was wearing a blushing pink, embroidered poshak, and he felt his heart skip a beat when he saw how resplendent she looked. She was flanked by Nirmal and three younger girls on one side, and by the senior ladies of the zenana on the other side. At that moment, though, Raj Singh hardly noticed anyone else. The sound of the nagaras grew louder as he approached the steps where she was standing, and then before she knew it, they were face to face. It had been many weeks, but it seemed more like an eternity to her. An eternity of praying and waiting for him to return. Now, even as she smeared his forehead with a red tilak and rotated the thaali three times as per tradition, their eyes met and he extended his right hand, palm facing up. And then, reading his mind as perfectly as she knew her own, Charumati handed the thaali over to Nirmal, revealing what had been concealed under it. There it was, hidden away beneath the folds of her odhni, the painting of Lord Krishna and Princess Rukmani that she had waited so long to give him.

She offered the painting to him. It had been thoroughly cleaned and polished since the last time he had seen it, and now every hue, every outline, every corner of its frame, shone and shimmered. Accepting it, he touched it to his forehead as a mark of reverence and then smiled at her. "Do you know the strangest thing?"

"What?"

"That our story started with a painting and has now been concluded with a painting too."

"That is indeed very strange." Charumati stared at him in wonder. "I never even thought of that."

"Well, I hope you have done what I had requested you to do. Have you found the perfect spot for it?" He raised his eyebrows enquiringly.

"Yes, I have." She nodded. "I cannot wait to show it to you."

"Shall we go inside then?"

Even above the din of the dhols and nagaras, he could distinctly hear the tinkle of her silver anklets as Charumati stepped to the side and waved her hand toward the palace door. "*Padharo,* Rana ji. Padharo."

Then, amidst a shower of rose and marigold petals, surrounded by scores of ladies performing a celebratory ghoomar, and thousands of people shouting out their blessings, Princess Charumati and Rana Raj Singh smiled at each other and walked through the double doors of the illuminated palace.

EPILOGUE

Rana Raj Singh and Princess Charumati got married[94] at the Raj Mahal palace in Udaipur soon after the victorious Rajput force returned. The wedding took place in the presence and with the blessings of Charumati's brother and other members of the Kishengarh and Udaipur royal families.

The most heart-breaking outcome of the war of 1660 that occurred between the Rajputs and the Mughals was the tragic demise of Rani Sahal Kanwar (also known as Hadi Rani) and her husband, the brave chieftain of the Chundawat clan, Rawat Ratan Singh Chundawat. As predicted by those who witnessed this true story, the names of Rawat Ratan Singh Chundawat and Hadi Rani have gone down in the pages of history. In fact, even today, people across Rajasthan worship this brave couple. Folklore singers tell their story through their music and Hadi Rani has inspired innumerable works of art. The tale is actually also a part of the curriculum of the state and as a sign of hailing her courage and fortitude, Rajasthan Police's first armed all women's battalion is named after the queen.[95]

Charumati's candid expression of affection and admiration for the Rana and her complete devotion to him, was not surprising to anyone. She had been in love with him much before the incident with

Aurangzeb compelled her to write to him. However, at a time when everyone, including her own brother, was fearful of standing up to the Mughal emperor, Raj Singh came to her help without a moment's hesitation. That also, was not astonishing since Mewar was one of the few states that had historically, valiantly stood up against enemy infiltration. Mewar's martial history in fact, had started as early as the eighth century during the invasion by the Arab caliphate, Muhammad Bin Qasim. His desire to conquer India was shattered after the humiliating defeat that he suffered at the hands of Mewar. It was this historic event that also set the base for what would go on to become a truly glorious legacy. A legacy that every Mewari ruler was palpably proud of. Raj Singh too upheld that legacy until his last breath. Suffice it to say that such was the extent of his indomitable reputation that Chattrapati Shivaji Maharaj once even taunted Aurangzeb by challenging him to collect the infamous Jizya tax from Maharana Raj Singh if he had the courage, instead of terrorizing unarmed civilians. Just as his great-great-grandfather Maharana Pratap had been a source of constant frustration and obstruction for Akbar during his reign, so was Raj Singh for Aurangzeb.

Raj Singh succeeded to the gaddi in the year 1652 but was crowned only in 1654. From the outset it was clear that his reign would bring about a paradigm shift in the position, autonomy and supremacy of Mewar. This change was even more strategically significant, considering the delicately balanced relationship between Delhi and Mewar.[96]

One of the first things that Raj Singh did after his succession was to push ahead the repair of Chittorgarh Fort. This was an extremely bold step. One of the conditions of the settlement that had occurred between Jehangir and Amar Singh in 1615 was that the walls of Chittor Fort were not to be repaired. Its ruined battlements would stand as a symbol of Mughal victory and dominance. Re-fortifying the fort meant breaching the treaty, and this obviously did not go down well with Shah Jahan. As far as Raj Singh was concerned, the step was representative of the revived glory of Mewar.[97] And it was just the beginning.

During the period of the Civil War between Aurangzeb and his brother Dara, Raj Singh used tactical negotiation and assertion to recover lost kingdoms and renew claims. In fact, over the next few years, he did not hesitate from striking Mughal posts when required because his sole aim was to firmly establish Mewar's military prowess in the region.

It is therefore clear that a man as resolute and principled as Rana Raj Singh would not have hesitated even for an instant when the woman he loved sought his help. His decision was made as soon as he received Charumati's letter to come and save her from being taken to Delhi on that fateful day. His military expertise and competence were evident from the way he led his army to victory, despite not being in an advantageous position as far as time and the size of the contingent were concerned.

The *jizya* or *kharāj* tax was another source of agitation between Aurangzeb and Raj Singh.[98] In India, the Jizya was introduced by Ahmad Shah of Gujarat in the year 1414 and was later abolished by Akbar in 1579. In the year 1679, Aurangzeb decided to reimpose the tax, a decision that was tenaciously and vociferously opposed by Raj Singh. He was actually one of the very few rulers who had the courage to stand up in public against the reimposition of the tax.

The year 1679 was actually strategically significant for the Mewar Mughal relationship for more reasons than one. Other than the re-imposition of the Jizya, the year also marked the death of Jaswant Singh of Marwar. The demise of the Rathore Rajput ruler set in motion a series of events which ultimately led to a conflict between Aurangzeb and Raj Singh. It all started with Aurangzeb attempting to interfere in the succession of Marwar. Durgadas Rathore who was a Rajput general in the army of Jaswant Singh started a campaign of resistance against Mughal interference in their internal matters.[99] When Durgadas and other members of the royal family of Marwar sought refuge in Raj Singh's court, he immediately came to their aid. This was the beginning of the first Rathore-Sisodia alliance. Despite Aurangzeb sending multiple letters to Raj Singh, asking that the conflict be resolved through negotiation, Raj Singh refused to bow down to any of the emperor's demands.[100] This led to the Rajput war which went on for twenty-eight long years, finally resulting in the triumphant capture of Jodhpur by the Rathores.

Apart from being a formidable force on the battlefield, Raj Singh was also a wonderful administrator and a great patron of music, literature, art and architecture.[101] In 1669, he ordered the construction of shrines to house the idols of Shri Nath ji[102] and Shri Dwarkanath ji in perpetuity. Raj Singh and his wife Charumati are also credited with building the Raisamand Lake also known as the Rajsamudra Lake between the cities of Rajnagar and Kankroli in the year 1676.[103] A Sanskrit text and inscription commissioned by the Rana, commemorated the construction of this water body. This text was authored by Ranchhod Bhatt Tailang and titled *'The Raj Prashasti'.* It was later inscribed on the stone slabs around the lake. This strategically important lake was used as a landing base for sea planes prior to India's independence and has over the years, acted as a critical water source for famine-stricken parts as also for farmers in the area.

Raj Singh 1 of the Sisodia Rajput dynasty was the eldest son of Maharana Jagat Singh and the Princess of Marwar and one of the longest reigning rulers of Mewar. His reign undoubtedly marked a tremendous shift in the dynamics of prestige and power in Delhi and Rajputana during the seventeenth century. This brave Maharana who did not once shy away from taking hard decisions, who unfailingly stood up for what was right, defying and resisting the mightiest forces, daring to do what others couldn't have even imagined, was a man of unquestionable honour and integrity. A man who was as tenacious and determined as he was benevolent and noble, Raj Singh 1 was a revered ruler, a true leader whose sole aim was to uphold and defend the glorious legacy of his homeland, Mewar.

ENDNOTES

1. Chand, Nihal. The Gundalao Lake. The Collection. Asian Art. The Metropolitan Museum of Art.
2. Molly Emma Aitken. Purdah and Portrayal – Rajput Women as Subjects, Patrons and Collectors. Artibus Asiae Publishers.
3. Cleaveland, Milo. The Context of Rajput Painting. Ars Orientalis, Vol 10 (1975), pp 11-17
4. Shahjahanabad (Old Delhi). India Habitat Center. Habitat Library and Resource Center.
5. Interview with Dr. Shankar Kumar. Noted Historian. Hindu College, Delhi University. January 2024.
6. Eaton, Richard M. Aurangzeb – From Prince to Emperor 'Alamgir. India in the Persianate Age 1000-1765. Allen Lane.
7. Interview with Diwan Gautam Anand. Famed Sufi poet, columnist and hotelier. September 2023.
8. Eaton, Richard M. Aurangzeb – From Prince to Emperor 'Alamgir'. India in the Persianate Age 1000-1765. Allen Lane.
9. Zaman. Taymiya R. A Hindu Soldier's Aurangzeb. University of San Fransisco. College of Arts and Sciences.
10. Interview with Dr. Shankar Kumar. Noted Historian. Hindu College, Delhi University. January 2024.
11. Interview with Dr. Shankar Kumar. Noted Historian. Hindu College, Delhi University. January 2024.
12. Husain, Afzal. Marriages among Mughal nobles as an index of status and aristocratic integration. Proceedings of the Indian History Congress. Vol 33 (1971), pp 304-312. Indian History Congress.
13. Mukhoty, Ira. The making of Akbar's complicated harem. Scroll. 29th April 2020.
14. Dutta, Parshati. Cultural heritage conservation consultant. The Mughal imperial road. 29th August 2018.
15. Interview with Rajendra Singh. Registered with Ministry of Tourism, Govt of India and Archaeological Survey of India.
16. Tauseef, Khadija. Princess Zeb-un-nissa. Rebel Sufi poetess and her gilded garden prison. Ancient Origins. 4th March 2021.
17. Interview with Diwan Gautam Anand. Famed Sufi poet, columnist and hotelier. September 2023.

18 Interview with Dr. Shankar Kumar. Noted Historian. Hindu College, Delhi University. January 2024.

19 Women at the Mughal Court: Perception and Reality. Francesca Galloway Art Gallery. London, UK.

20 Interview with Diwan Gautam Anand. Famed Sufi poet, columnist and hotelier. September, 2023.

21 Women at the Mughal Court: Perception and Reality. Francesca Galloway Art Gallery. London, UK.

22 Tauseef, Khadija. Princess Zeb-un-nissa. Rebel Sufi poetess and her gilded garden prison. Ancient Origins. 4 March 2021.

23 Interview with Diwan Gautam Anand. Famed Sufi poet, columnist and hotelier. September 2023.

24 Interview with Dr. Shankar Kumar. Noted Historian. Hindu College, Delhi University. January 2024.

25 A Game of Thrones. How chess conquered the world. Archives from the Salar Jung Museum.

26 Honchell, Stephanie. Pursuing pleasure, attaining oblivion: the roles and uses of intoxicants at the Mughal court. Theses and Dissertations. University of Louisville. 1984.

27 Interview with Dr. Shankar Kumar. Noted Historian. Hindu College, Delhi University. January 2024.

28 Zaman, Taymiya R. A Hindu Soldier's Aurangzeb. The Wire. 15th January, 2016.

29 Moghadam, M.E. A note on the etymology of the word checkmate. Journal of the American Oriental Society. Vol 58, No 4 (Dec 1938), pp 662-664. American Oriental Society.

30 Tola, Maya M. The decline of Mughal arts under Aurangzeb. Daily Art. 7th September, 2023.

31 Begum Zeb-un-nissa. A Princess Unchained. Archives from The Rekhta Foundation. Devoted to the preservation and promotion of Urdu Language, Literature & Culture.

32 Tauseef, Khadija. Princess Zeb-un-nissa. Rebel Sufi poetess and her gilded garden prison. Ancient Origins. 4 March 2021.

33 Aitken, Molly Emma. Pardah and Portrayal: Rajput Women as Subjects, Patrons and Collectors. Artibus Asiae, Vol 62, No. 2, 2002, pp 247-280.

34 Eaton, Richard M. Aurangzeb – From Prince to Emperor 'Alamgir. India in the Persianate Age 1000-1765. Allen Lane.

35 Liddle, Swapna. This is how Delhi reacted to Aurangzeb's killing of Dara Shukoh. Feb, 16th, 2017. Hindustan Times.

36 Mathur, M.M. Glorious Mewar. Bulletin of the Deccam College Post-Graduate and Research Institute, Vol 68/69 (2008-2009) pp-277-292

37 Nahar Singh, Rawat II. Rajasthani Painters. Bagta and Chokha. Master Artists at Devgarh. Artibus Asiae. Supplementum. Vol 46.

38 Gupta, K.S. Maratha Expansion and Rajput Resistance. Proceedings of the Indian History Congress. Vol 32. Vol II (1970) pp 32-37

39 Husain, Afzal. Marriages among Mughal nobles as an index of status and aristocratic integration. Proceedings of the Indian History Congress, Vol 33 (1971), pp 304-312.

40 Aitken, Molly Emma. Pardah and Portrayal: Rajput women as subjects, patrons and collectors. Artibus Asiae. Volume. 62, No 2 (2002), pp 247 – 280. Artibus Asiae Publishers.

41 Mukhoty, Ira. The making of Akbar's complicated harem. Scroll. 29th April 2020.

42 Rumi. Dance when you're broken open. Translated by Coleman Barks. With John Moyne. Penguin Arkana.

43 Irfan, Lubna. Aligarh Muslim University. Third Gender and Service in Mughal Court and Harem. Servants Pasts. European Research Council Project, 2015-18.

44 Butler Brown, Katherine. Did Aurangzeb ban Music? Questions for the Historiography of his Reign. Modern Asian Studies. Vol 41, No. 1. (Jan 2007), pp 77-120. Cambridge University Press.

45 Arnold David, Toxic Histories, The social life of poisons, 5th February, 2016, Cambridge University Press.

46 Armour, W.S. Customs of Warfare in Ancient India. Vol 8, Problems of Peace and War, Papers read before the society in the year 1922 (1922) pp 71-88. Cambridge University Press.

47 Mathur, M.M. Glorious Mewar. Bulletin of the Deccan College Post-Graduate and Research Institute. Vol 86, 69 (2008-2009), pp 227 – 292.

48 Elephant Stories, Miniature Paintings from Mughal India. Staatliche Museen Zu Berlin.

49 Prince Awrangzeb facing a maddened elephant named Sudhaka (7th June 1633). 1656-57. Royal Collection Trust.

50 Wigh, Sonia. Politics, Patronage and Polyvalence: Mirza Raja Jai Singh in Biharilal's Satsai. Social Scientist, Vol 43, No. 5/6 (May-June 2015) pp 47-64

51 Anecdotes of Aurangzeb and Historical Essays. Works by Prof. Jadunath Sarkar. Institute of Islamic Studies. Rare Books Society of India.

52 Butler Brown, Katherine. Did Aurangzeb ban Music? Questions for the Historiography of his Reign. Modern Asian Studies. Vol 41, No. 1. (Jan 2007), pp 77-120. Cambridge University Press.

53 Anecdotes of Aurangzeb and Historical Essays. Works by Prof. Jadunath Sarkar. Institute of Islamic Studies. Rare Books Society of India.

54 Jehangir Embracing Shah Abbas. National Museum of Asian Art.

55 Anecdotes of Aurangzeb and Historical Essays. Works by Prof. Jadunath Sarkar. Institute of Islamic Studies. Rare Books Society of India.

56 Interview with Diwan Gautam Anand. Famed Sufi poet, columnist and hotelier. September 2023.

57 Interview with Rajendra Singh. Registered Guide with Ministry of Tourism, Govt of India and Archaeological Survey of India.

58 Ul Haque, Inam. Mughal Army and Royalty. 17th November, 2022. The Tribune.

59 Shafqat, Arshia. Public Face of the Mughal Empire-The Proceedings of the Diwan-i-Khas o Aam. Proceedings of the Indian History Congress. Vol 73 (2012), pp 241-248.

60 Wigh, Sonia. Politics, Patronage and Polyvalence: Mirza Raja Jai Singh in Biharilal's Satsai. Social Scientist Vol 43, No. 5/6 (May – June 2015), pp 47-64.

61 Kumar, Anu. The Brahman in the Mughal Court. The Wire. 15th November 2016.

62 Eaton, Richard M. Aurangzeb – From Prince to Emperor 'Alamgir. India in the Persianate Age 1000-1765. Allen Lane.

63 Malecka, Anna. Solar Symbolism of the Mughal Thrones. Arts Asiatiques, Vol 54 (1999), pp 24-32.

64 B.K. Athira. Bridal Ornamentation and Gender Performances in India: A Literature Review. Indian Anthropologist. Vol. 52, No.1/2. (January to December 2022), pp 139-153

65 Chapter 2. Religion and Rajput Women. UC Press E-Books Collection 1982-2004. University of California Press.

66 Interview with Salma Yusuf Husain. Food Historian and Persian Scholar.

67 Hooja, Rima. Maharana Pratap. Juggernaut. January, 2019.

68 Maharana Pratap's Guerilla Warfare. Medium. 8th July, 2020.

69 A Maze in a Stepwell. Chand Baori. Rajasthan Tourism. Government

of India.

70 Fatma, Sadaf. Gardens in Mughal Gujarat. Proceedings of the Indian History Congress. Vol 72, Part 1, (2011), pp 441-452.

71 Bano, Shadab. Eunuchs in Mughal Household and Court. Proceedings of the Indian History Congress, Vol 69 (2008), pp 417-427

72 Chandra, Satish. A re-examination of the factors leading to the breach between Aurangzib and Rana Raj Singh. Proceedings of the Indian History Congress. Vol 27 (1965) pp 169-176.

73 Sahu, Monideepa. Royal Portrait. Deccan Herald. 4th August, 2012.

74 Red Fort. The Mughal Imperial Citadel. Indian National Trust for Art and Culture Heritage (Delhi Chapter)

75 Jag Mandir Palace. Heritage. Incredible India.

76 Agre, Jagat Vir Singh. Social Life as Reflected in the Rajput Painting during the Mughal Period. Proceedings of the Indian History Congress, Vol 37 (1976), pp 569-575.

77 Aitken, Molly Emma. Pardah and Portrayal: Rajput Women as Subjects, Patrons and Collectors. Artibus Asiae, Vol 62, No. 2, 2002, pp 247-280.

78 B.K. Athira. Bridal Ornamentation and Gender Performances in India: A Literature Review. Indian Anthropologist. Vol. 52, No.1/2. (January to December 2022), pp 139-153

79 Genealogy and Identity. Rajasthan and the Rajputs. Religion and Rajput Women. University of California Press.

80 Armour, W.S. Customs of Warfare in Ancient India. Transactions of the Grotius Society. Vol 8, Problems of Peace and War. Papers Read before the Society in the Year 1922, pp 71-88. Cambridge University Press.

81 Sharma, Ravindra Kumar. The Military System of the Mewar (Udaipur) State. (Ca. 800 to 1947 AD). Central Asiatic Journal, Vol 30, No. ½ (1986), pp 116-140

82 Sharma, Ravindra Kumar. The Military System of the Mewar (Udaipur) State. (Ca. 800 to 1947 AD). Central Asiatic Journal, Vol 30, No. ½ (1986), pp 116-140

83 Military System of the Mughals. Chapter 6. The National Institute of Open Schooling. Ministry of Education. Government of India.

84 Husain, Iqbal. Some Afghan Settlement in the Gangetic Doab 1627-1707. Proceedings of the Indian History Congress, Vol 31 (1969), pp 173-181.

85 Husain, Afzal. Afghan nobility under Akbar and Jahangir – The family of Daulat Khan Lodi. Proceedings of the Indian History Congress, Vol 48

(1987), pp . 187 – 196.

86 The decapitation of Khan Jahan Lodi (3rd February, 1631). C 1635-1650. Royal Collection Trust, UK.

87 Mathur, M.M. Glorious Mewar. Bulletin of the Deccan College Post Graduate and Research Institute, Vol 68/69 (2008-2009), pp 277-292

88 Honchell Smith, Stephanie. Aurangzeb, Mughal Emperor. Origins, Current Events in Historical Perspective. Ohio State University.

89 Smith, John D. Religion and Rajput Women: The Ethic of Protection in Contemporary Narratives by Lindsey Harlan. Modern Asian Studies Vol 29, No. 1 (Feb 1995) pp 223-224

90 Ganesh, Sandhya. The Tale of Headless Love. Medium. 27th August, 2020.

91 Kumar, Arjun. Aesthetic way of dealing with heat in Medieval India. The Economic Times. 7th May 2009.

92 Interview with Salma Yusuf Husain Noted Persian scholar and historian.

93 Sengar, Resham. Hadi Rani Ki Baori. 14th June, 2019. The Times of India.

94 Zaidi, S. Inayat Ali. The Pattern of Matrimonial Ties between the Kachawaha Clan and the Mughal Ruling Family. Proceedings of the Indian History Congress, Vol 35 (1974), pp131-143.

95 Inamdar, Manisha. Hadi Rani. Story of Courage and Sacrifice. History, Trunicle. 18th March, 2021.

96 Rana Raj Singh 1. The Indian Portrait. An online museum on the fascinating journey of India Portraits from the collection of Indian Art Collector, Anil Relia.

97 Chandra, Satish. A re-examination of the factors leading to the breach between Aurangzeb and Rana Raj Singh. Proceedings of the Indian History Congress, Vol 27 (1965), pp 169-176.

98 Mathur, M.M. Glorious Mewar. Bulletin of the Deccan College Post-Graduate and Research Institute, Vol 68-69 (2008-2009), pp 277-292.

99 Eaton, Richard M. Aurangzeb – From Prince to Emperor 'Alamgir. India in the Persianate Age 1000-1765. Allen Lane.

100 Mewar Mughal Relations. Mughal Polity. Dissertation. BA Hons (History) University of Delhi.

101 Raj Singh. Hindustan Times. 24th September, 2021.

102 Harlan, Lindsey. Aurangzeb: Stories from Mewar. 23rd European Conference on South Asian Studies.

103 Mathur, M.M. Glorious Mewar. Bulletin of the Deccan College Post-Graduate and Research Institute, Vol 68-69 (2008-2009), pp 277-292.

By the Same Author

The Royal Scandal